Past Masters
General Editor Ke

Johnson

Past Masters

Forthcoming

Pat Rogers

Johnson

Oxford   New York

OXFORD UNIVERSITY PRESS

1993

Oxford University Press, Walton Street, Oxford OX2 6DP

Oxford New York Toronto
Delhi Bombay Calcutta Madras Karachi
Kuala Lumpur Singapore Hong Kong Tokyo
Nairobi Dar es Salaam Cape Town
Melbourne Auckland Madrid

and associated companies in
Berlin Ibadan

Oxford is a trade mark of Oxford University Press

First published 1993 as an Oxford University Press paperback

British Library Cataloguing in Publication Data
Data available

Library of Congress Cataloging in Publication Data
Rogers, Pat.
Johnson / Pat Rogers.
p. cm.
1. Johnson, Samuel, 1709–1784. 2. Great Britain—Intellectual
life—18th century. 3. Authors, English—18th century—Biography.
4. Lexicographers—Great Britain—Biography. 5. Critics—Great
Britain—Biography. I. Title.
828'.609—dc20 PR3533.R63 1993 [B] 92–25832
ISBN 0–19–287593–0

1 3 5 7 9 10 8 6 4 2

Typeset by Best-Set Typesetter Ltd.
Printed in Great Britain by
Biddles Ltd.,
Guildford and King's Lynn

Preface

One of the best-known stories of Johnson is told by Boswell, and concerns Goldsmith's remark that the Club needed new members, 'for (said he), there can be nothing new among us: we have travelled over one another's minds. Johnson seemed a little angry, and said, "Sir, you have not travelled over *my* mind, I promise you"' (B 4. 183). It would be a vain author who expected to travel all over Johnson's mind in a little more than a hundred pages. My aims are more modest. They are to offer some indication of the scope of Johnson's contribution to ideas; to try to define his importance within his own age; to quote his work freely, so as to give the flavour of his mind; and to suggest the reasons for his lasting interest. I have also drawn on contemporaries who knew Johnson personally, a boon which can never be ours. Above all, I hope that this book will send readers back to Johnson's own work, which is where they will make their own discoveries.

Acknowledgements

The epigraph on p. 28 is taken from Saul Bellow, *Mr Sammler's Planet*, published by Penguin Books, copyright Saul Bellow, 1969. I am grateful to the publishers for permission to reprint.

Short passages of Chapter 6 constitute a revised version of material which originally appeared in my essay, 'Dr Johnson and the English Language', in *Oxford English: A Guide to the Language*, ed. I. C. B. Dear (Oxford, 1986). Again, I acknowledge with gratitude permission to use this material.

Contents

for Donald Greene
Opposition is true friendship

Abbreviations

Short forms are used in the text as indicated below (place of publication is London, unless otherwise shown). In general, spelling and typography have been brought into line with modern usage, but punctuation left undisturbed. Periodical essays such as the *Rambler* are cited by number rather than page reference.

Johnson's works

L   *The Letters of Samuel Johnson*, ed. R. W. Chapman, 3 vols. (Oxford, 1952)

LOP   *The Lives of the Poets*, ed. G. B. Hill, 3 vols. (Oxford, 1905)

W   *The Works of Samuel Johnson, L.D.*, ed. Arthur Murphy, 12 vols. (1792, repr. 1823)

Y   *The Yale Edition of the Works of Samuel Johnson*, ed. A. T. Hazen, J. H. Middledorf, *et al.*, 13 vols. (New Haven, Conn., 1958–   )

Other Sources

A   Hester Piozzi, *Anecdotes of the late Samuel Johnson*, ed. A. Sherbo (1974)

B   James Boswell, *The Life of Samuel Johnson*, ed. G. B. Hill and L. F. Powell, 6 vols. (Oxford, 1934–64)

D&L   *The Diary and Letters of Madame d'Arblay*, ed. C. Barrett, 7 vols. (1842–7)

H   John Hawkins, *The Life of Samuel Johnson, LL.D.*, ed. B. H. Davis (1961)

JM   *Johnsonian Miscellanies*, ed. G. B. Hill, 2 vols. (Oxford, 1897)

T   *Thraliana: The Diary of Mrs Hester Lynch Thrale*, ed. K. C. Balderston, 2 vols. (Oxford, 2nd edn., 1951)

1 Introduction

Neither Johnson himself, nor his contemporaries, would have felt much surprise to find him ranged among the Past Masters. Unlike several figures included in this series, he was recognized in his own day as something more than a considerable writer: he was a sage. The variety of nicknames bestowed on him, and their currency, testify to this fact: the Great Cham, and so on. We do not speak commonly of the Age of Newton, even though the great scientist's influence extended far beyond the technical sphere of cosmography or physics, but we do speak of the Age of Johnson, and with good reason. No one has a higher visibility in mid-Hanoverian culture, and no one embodies so fully the temper of his time. Crotchety and individualistic, even isolated, in his private circumstances, backward-looking and ultra-orthodox in many of his opinions, Samuel Johnson nevertheless bestrode his epoch as no other English man or woman quite managed to do— and his nearest rivals would include friends and fellow Club members such as Burke and Gibbon. To find an equivalent impress upon the age, we must look to another country (Voltaire) or to another century (Freud). He has acquired a historical persona which goes beyond his narrowly literary achievement, and that process started within his own lifetime.

It follows that any account of Johnson today must draw in many intellectual threads and explore many fibres of cultural life. The aim of this book is to give a general survey of Johnson's contribution to ideas, and this must rely chiefly on a descriptive analysis of what Johnson actually wrote. But first we need to look briefly at Johnson's position in his own age, and to see why he stood out as the grand panjandrum in a company by no means bereft of high distinction in the arts, philosophy, and the social sciences. Indeed, it is only when we set Johnson alongside his eminent contemporaries that we begin to isolate his special powers and identify the peculiar resonance of his mind. This introductory chapter will, therefore, consider him in relation to his colleagues and friends (with a few enemies): these were people equal or close to him in magnitude within their own sphere, but they do not approach Johnson as a central symbol of their times. They have a reputation: he has become a myth. Several were writers of the highest talent; only Johnson qualified for the role in which he was cast by Thomas Carlyle, the man of letters as hero of early modern times.

Johnson has suffered from the fact that he wrote so widely, across the whole span of literature. We may think that people in the past—not least the Augustans—were obsessed by the literary kinds, but in truth it is our own age which has become fixated on genre. Only in recent years has the history of literature been written, not as a procession of great creators and great ideas, but as a running battle between different genres in competition for dominance. Johnson belonged to a world where professional writers who could not do several things scarcely got the chance to do one. He was clearly proud of his ability to move freely from one task to another; what he valued was a general power of the mind, rather than any highly specific technique or method of approach. The tributes of contemporaries like Reynolds, Burke, and Boswell show that they felt they had been educated by the scope of Johnson's mental energy and precision. For example, when Reynolds wrote: 'He may be said to have formed my mind, and to have brushed from it a deal of rubbish' (JM 2. 227), he was alluding to Johnson's capacity to teach people 'to think rightly'. He did not mean that Johnson had given him a course in literature, though directed reading was certainly on the programme. Reynolds was referring to the way in which his friend's free-ranging discourse (in conversation as in print) opened up new vistas—the *Rambler* by itself contains satire, moralizing, fantasy, fiction, social criticism, literary theory, philosophic commentary, and much else.

It is important, then, to attend to Johnson in every mood. There is no hard-and-fast divide between the published writing and the conversational or anecdotal evidence. Of course, the peak of his achievement is to be found in his very greatest books, including the *Dictionary*, the *Rambler*, the *Journey to the Western Islands*, and the *Lives of the Poets*. But it is an illusion to suppose that every verdict delivered in those *Lives* is pondered and 'serious', whereas comments on the same writers in the course of oral discussion are casual and shallow. It happens, too, that Johnson's intellectual life was chronicled by some of the shrewdest observers who could possibly have been found: Boswell, Fanny Burney, and Hester Thrale principally, but also a long list of part-time anecdotalists such as Joshua Reynolds, Edmond Malone, and Hannah More. Even his enemies were worth having: Lord Chesterfield, Thomas Gray, David Hume, Rousseau. He impressed, charmed, and provoked people as diverse as John Wilkes, Pasquale Paoli, Elizabeth Carter, Charles James Fox, Sarah Siddons, and Warren Hastings. He was the object of an unparalleled degree of scrutiny, because he was recognized by so many as a man of exceptional human, as well as intellectual, interest; it is no accident that he wrote the first serious psychological biography in the language (that of Richard Savage), and was the subject of the first truly profound life of a writer's mind (that of Boswell). As a matter of fact, he inspired from Sir John Hawkins, before Hester Thrale and Boswell had brought out their own works, a biography which would otherwise endure as one of the outstanding examples of the genre which had ever appeared up to that time. The wealth of Johnsoniana is not a sign of misplaced energy, mere gossip substituting for intelligent discussion; it reflects the natural and justified public attention which Johnson's career drew.

Although Johnson had little time for the *philosophes*, he belongs in one obvious sense to the Age of Enlightenment. With his *Dictionary*, he brought unprecedented order and method to the study of the English language, even as the great French *Encyclopédie* had ranged the corpus of human knowledge into alphabetical sequence. His edition of Shakespeare did more than any other version, above all by its eloquent Preface, to confirm the dramatist as the greatest living classic of English literature. Finally, in his *Lives of the Poets* Johnson made the first coherent map of earlier poetic history. It was this work which originally set out an English canon, in an age which had no Modern Library or World's Classics. One might even claim that the very concept of an English classic only begins to make sense after the appearance of these *Lives*.

This codifying function was the purest expression of Enlightenment culture. Just how central Johnson's role was in this regard has been made clear by Lawrence Lipking in his study, *The Ordering of the Arts in Eighteenth-Century England* (1970). Lipking aligns the *Lives of the Poets* (1779–81) with Thomas Warton's *History of English Poetry* (1774–81) as the founding documents of literary history. Parallel contributions had been made to the history of music by Sir John Hawkins and Charles Burney, and to the study of the fine arts by Joshua Reynolds and Horace Walpole. A great collective enterprise, with Johnson at its centre, was essentially conducted by members of the Club—the Literary Club, or more openly Johnson's Club. Among the six authors named, only Horace Walpole stood aloof as a member of an oppositional group hostile to Club norms.

However, that is not the whole story. Other branches of knowledge were lent a similar impetus at the very same juncture by other luminaries in the Club. In 1776 Adam Smith had helped to found the science of political economy with *The Wealth of Nations*, whilst Gibbon had realigned the matter and manner of historiography (and not just for the ancient world) with his *Decline and Fall of the Roman Empire*. Meanwhile, Edmund Burke—who had already given the definitive aesthetic appraisal of the sublime and the beautiful—was reformulating the art of political rhetoric, in pamphlets and speeches, culminating in his *Reflections on the Revolution in France* (1790). A year later Boswell unexpectedly joined the list of great initiators with his *Life of Johnson*, which extended the compass and human penetration of biography as a form. Later in the 1790s came the pioneering editorial work of Edmond Malone, which not merely transformed the state of knowledge concerning Shakespeare in his own age but equally brought new standards of rigour to the activity of an editor. One might add that Garrick by his own practice had extended the vocabulary of the actor and had given a new dignity to the profession, whilst Charles James Fox and Richard Brinsley Sheridan had outdone even Burke in the sphere of parliamentary oratory. All these men were members of the Club, and it was Johnson who stood as the keystone in all Club doings.

Of course, there were other contemporaries who promoted this burst in the advancement in learning. There were figures excluded from the Club, for one reason or another. Some leaders of the

Scottish Enlightenment such as David Hume would have been too radical in their views, on religion especially; others, such as Adam Ferguson, the founder of sociology, seldom went anywhere near London anyway. Others in the line of the pioneer neurologist Robert Whytt were simply too much hard scientists to be able to earn ready admission to a humanist group like the Club. Another segment of the population, women, were excluded purely on grounds of sex; none the less, the great actress Sarah Siddons, the distinguished novelist Fanny Burney, the social reformer Hannah More, the scholar Elizabeth Carter, and the remarkable woman of letters Hester Thrale all stood on the edge of the Club, with many firsthand contacts and alliances. Indeed, it is possible to chart an extensive overlap between the habitués, male and female, of the salons conducted by women such as Elizabeth Montagu and the immediate Johnson circle.

In suggesting that almost all lines of significant cultural force radiate out from Johnson and his group, I do not mean to indicate that he personally understood, or approved of, every single manifestation of this renaissance in knowledge. He knew little of the musical matters treated by his friend Charles Burney; he did not agree with all the theoretical positions implied in Burke's aesthetic of surprise and novelty; he probably did not care greatly either way when it came to the notional rankings of painters set out in Reynolds's *Discourses*. He was hospitable to some of the ideas of the new science of his time, no adversary to the classificatory ambitions of a Linnaeus, and possessed an amateur interest in medicine. Another of the Club illuminati was Joseph Banks, whose accounts of his Pacific discoveries on Cook's first expedition certainly caught Johnson's imagination, and this does not apply just to his evident fascination with the kangaroo. Nevertheless, it could not be said that Johnson was fully acquainted with the advances in science of his time, for example in what we should call physics.

The claim which can be sustained for Johnson is that he took a wide interest in a far more extensive sweep of human knowledge than anybody is likely to pursue today. Moreover, he brought to each subject a sense of the need for theoretical and methodical clarity. It is the task of criticism, he writes in *Rambler* 92 (Y 4. 122), 'to establish principles; to improve opinion into knowledge;

and to distinguish those means of pleasing which depend on known causes and rational deducation, from the nameless and inexplicable elegancies which appeal wholly to the fancy, from which we feel delight, but know not how they produce it... Criticism reduces those regions of literature under the dominion of science, which have hitherto known only the anarchy of ignorance, the caprices of fancy, and the tyranny of prescription.' This is as hard and positivist a line as anything in Diderot or d'Alembert at their most zealously encyclopaedic. If one sought a brief definition of Enlightenment goals, then the destruction of the anarchy of ignorance, the rejection of the caprices of fancy, and the conquest of the tyranny of prescription would serve very well.

Johnson had reached this position, not because he had given his days and nights to the modern bibles of French rationalism, but because of a background in older habits of thought. He possessed a sceptical and even dry intellect; he studied classical literature and its scholiasts, he perused the Christian Fathers, and he knew a great wealth of Renaissance learning. His cast of mind led him towards the central critical task of discrimination. Boswell cites Reynolds, as a figure with his own 'philosophical penetration and justness of thinking', on the way Johnson's views regarding his own friends derived from a particular mental pattern: 'He was fond of discrimination, which he could not show without pointing out the bad as well as the good in every character; and as his friends were those whose characters he knew best, they afforded him the best opportunity for showing the acuteness of his judgement' (B 2. 306). Johnson had grown up in the high moment of Augustan critical thought, when discrimination was allied with sound judgement against dangerous and capricious wit. Judgement had been described by a writer whom Johnson had read, Obadiah Walker, as 'the deliberate weighing and comparing of one object, one appearance, one reason with another, thereby to discern and choose true from false, good from bad, and more true and good from lesser'. It is this mode of discernment that Johnson habitually practised. We can see it in his moral essays, in his critical works, in his books of cultural analysis (such as the *Journey to the Western Islands of Scotland*), and regularly in his conversation as reported by the biographers.

Naturally, Johnson was well aware that 'human experience, which is constantly contradicting theory, is the great test of truth' (B 1. 454); hence his consuming passion for biography and for the realistic particularities which it offered up to confront general maxims. But theory here means something like empty speculation, rather than a solid review of the principles underlying an issue. It was Johnson's desire to sort out such overriding principles in the art of poetry which gives a substance to the particular readings offered in the *Lives of the Poets*; and it was a search for the stable foundations of language (however illusory they might prove) which united the thousands of separate entries in the *Dictionary*. Johnson had set out, for example, to apply a consistent policy on spelling English words, where 'caprice has long wandered without control' (W 10. 36). Johnson is thoroughly at one with most educated people of his time in retaining a faith in the ability of the mind to make sense of disparate phenomena by processes of collecting, sorting, filing, and redistributing. These routine, and as it were secular, operations of the mind were to lose influence dramatically when the Romantics revalued the imagination and devalued other cognitive functions.

2 Events

Externally Samuel Johnson led a fairly simple life. He spent his childhood and youth in the West Midlands, and the rest of his days in London, with few travels and no extensive period spent abroad. His adventures were those of the spirit.

He was born in Lichfield on 7 September 1709. He later celebrated his birthday on 18 September, after the change to the Gregorian calendar in 1752 meant dropping eleven days from that year. Queen Anne was on the throne (three years later young Samuel was taken to London to be 'touched' for his scrofula); by the time he reached the age of 5, the first Hanoverian, George I, had acceded. His parents, Michael and Sarah (neé Ford), were already into late middle age; Michael was a local worthy, probably a High Churchman and royalist, but not altogether a good businessman—his ventures as a bookseller, binder, and publisher were moderately prosperous, but he diversified into running a parchment factory and the combined enterprise failed: when Michael died in 1731, at the age of 75, there was little money to pass on to his widow and son. One thing that he did bequeath to Samuel was a neurotic streak. He had at least built the solid four-storey house on the corner of the market place in Lichfield, where Samuel was born and which remains the centre-point of local piety as the site of a Johnson museum today.

Johnson began his education at a small dame school, and passed at the age of 7 to Lichfield Grammar School. The regime and curriculum were traditional, with a thorough grounding in Latin the first aim and in time the basis of Johnson's mastery of the intellectual map of mankind. In the upper school, which the youngster entered in 1719, he began the study of Greek under the formidable headmaster John Hunter, whose harsh discipline and brutal ways incurred Johnson's dislike. In 1725 he left Lichfield school, and spent a period with a dissipated and worldly clergyman cousin named Cornelius Ford, involving a spell at another grammar school in Stourbridge. Then followed a sojourn of idleness at home, until at 19 he was enabled to proceed to Pembroke College, Oxford, chiefly as a result of a subvention from an old schoolfellow at Lichfield who was now a gentleman commoner at Pembroke. It was always a financial strain, and as it turned out Johnson had to give up residence after little more than a year, in December 1729. He had been given a Pisgah vision of the good life as he no doubt conceived it—a world of books, scholarship, and late hours, of competitive talk and comparative freedom after the small-town atmosphere of Lichfield and *res angusti domi* in the bookshop— quite literally so, for it was a tall, narrow house.

Young Samuel was forced to return home with his dreams crushed, and spent some fruitless years in and around his home-town. He tried to make a career as a schoolmaster, setting up a school of his own outside Lichfield, where David Garrick was one of his few pupils; but the venture soon collapsed. After leaving Oxford, Johnson had suffered some kind of nervous breakdown, and his spirits cannot have lifted in the early 1730s as his father died and his worldly affairs showed no sign of improvement. Suddenly out of the blue (as it now looks to us), Johnson married a draper's widow from Birmingham named Elizabeth Porter. She was 46, twenty years Johnson's senior. We still know less about the marriage than about any other aspect of comparable importance in Johnson's life. Elizabeth, known as 'Tetty', became a stock joke with his friends; early biographers were not kind to her, and Boswell was unable to find out very much which would explain the lasting affection Johnson evidently felt for his wife, despite some minor quarrels which seem to have been nothing more than the ordinary ups and downs of married life. In March 1737, two years after the marriage, Johnson went up to London with his former pupil David Garrick, but without Elizabeth. A few months later he made a trip home and then returned to London for good, this time with his wife; they lived in a succession of lodgings on the west side of London. The capital had a population of some six-hundred thousand, more than twenty times as large as Birmingham, the greatest metropolis Johnson had known until then. The main attraction of London was its position as the centre of the book-trade and the focus of the literary nation. The aspirant author's hopes were concentrated around his verse tragedy *Irene*, begun about 1736 and lingering on

9

as a lost cause until its production in 1749 finally convinced its author that it would not do.

Throughout the early years of Johnson's sojourn in London his chief support came from work on the *Gentleman's Magazine*, the first important literary journal in England. By this means he became acquainted with a large slice of the authorial profession in London, most notably the self-destructive bohemian poet Richard Savage, whose biography in 1744 was to be Johnson's first great book. Later, according to Arthur Murphy, Johnson would claim that he could give 'a better history of Grub Street than any man living' (JM 1. 414). Convincing evidence has recently shown that Johnson did not experience such dire poverty in these years as used to be thought, but it was certainly a hand-to-mouth existence for both husband and wife, with no luxuries and a constant pressure to maintain a secure livelihood. However, Johnson began to make a name, with translations, short biographies, and especially his satire *London*, which impressed the great arbiter of matters poetic, Alexander Pope. Both Pope and Swift were nearing the end of their lives, one in London, the other in Dublin; Johnson became an author just in time to feel their direct impress, and they remained crucial exemplars all through his career—though Pope was the recipient of a much friendlier treatment in the *Lives of the Poets* than Swift, whose unconventional attitudes in his role as a clergyman shocked Johnson, and whose sometimes nihilistic vision offended one who was trying with might and main to counter deep strains of pessimism in his own nature. If there is a direct heir to the great Scriblerian satirists, it is Johnson; but one is always conscious of a more tender and compassionate quality in him, fierce as his anger could be and implacably honest as his scrutiny of the dark side of life always remained.

'Slow rises worth, by poverty depressed', Johnson had written in *London*, capitalizing the line for added emphasis. His own career bore out the maxim, but eventually there were signs of an upturn. He began to compile the great *Dictionary* in 1746; after various changes of plan, he was able to complete this in 1755, and became famous as 'Dictionary Johnson'. By that time he had also produced his greatest poem, *The Vanity of Human Wishes* (1749), and his most characteristic single work, the series of *Rambler* papers which appeared twice-weekly between 1750 and 1752. He shared at one remove the success of Garrick, who had reached the pinnacle of his profession much earlier than his companion from Lichfield. Tetty Johnson died in 1752, and the widower embarked on the untidy bachelor existence in various London homes which was to be the pattern of the remainder of his life. He started to assemble around him the group of friends who would form the great constellation of talent making up the Johnson circle of later years. He met Reynolds, Goldsmith, Burke, and the Thrales; in 1763 the young Boswell engineered a meeting, and though Boswell soon afterwards left for his Grand Tour, the seeds had been sown of a relationship which was to provide our clearest glimpse of Johnson's day-to-day living. By this time Johnson had embarked on his edition of Shakespeare, which was to appear in 1765, and had written his second important set of periodical essays, those of the *Idler*. In 1759 Johnson's aged mother died, unvisited by her grieving but oddly detached son; in order to defray her funeral expenses, he quickly put together *Rasselas*, his only sustained work of prose fiction. Very gradually he was climbing out of the morass of Grub Street.

The last twenty-odd years of Johnson's life are the best known, and our usual image of his personality derives from this period. In 1762 he was awarded an annual pension of £300 by the young king, George III, more as a kind of official honour for services to literature than a payment for political duties, past or potential. In 1755 he had been awarded an MA by Oxford: again this was the equivalent not so much of a modern honorary degree as of an incorporation of some visiting scholar. In 1765 he received an honorary doctorate from Trinity College, Dublin, and in 1775 one from his old university. These were tangible signs of his recognized position at the head of English letters: his appointment as Professor of Ancient Literature when the Royal Academy was founded in 1768 reflects chiefly his support for the new institution and his friendship with its first president, Joshua Reynolds. It was Reynolds, too, who was behind the Literary Club, formed in 1764, the original members including Burke, Goldsmith, and Johnson's future biographer, Hawkins. Over time the Club was to expand and its membership came to embrace Garrick, Boswell, Adam Smith, Gibbon, Percy of the *Reliques*,

Charles James Fox, Sheridan, the Warton brothers, Dr Charles Burney, George Colman, Sir William Hamilton, Edmond Malone, and many other notable figures. We should not exaggerate the importance of this group, since its members had many other social and cultural ties—in Johnson's case with the circle of Mrs Thrale and then that of the Burneys, in other cases with parliamentary, painting, and theatrical sets. But it was assuredly the main locus of Johnson as a conversationalist for the last two decades of his life. He considered that social discourse was a serious part of a well-lived life, for a writer as for any other thinking being, and the stimulus he received from his bouts with the great company surrounding him ensured that he remained intellectually vital to the end.

This last phase saw the appearance of some political pamphlets in addition to a pair of his greatest works. The *Journey to the Western Islands* (1775) describes the tour he made with Boswell to the Highlands of Scotland and the Hebrides, two years earlier. Belatedly Johnson had begun to travel more; he paid visits with the Thrales to North Wales and then to Paris, although he was never able to make the voyage to Italy he had long contemplated. His financial circumstances were now better, but he maintained a household of poor dependants which placed a severe burden on his income. The last major work, the *Lives of the Poets*, was written as a set of prefaces to a booksellers' collection of earlier English poets. It appeared between 1779 and 1781; by now Johnson's health was failing, and his friends foresaw that his end could not be long delayed. His last months were clouded by a quarrel with his old and dear friend Hester Thrale, over her intended marriage to an Italian musician, Gabriel Piozzi. Boswell saw him for the last time on 30 June 1784, when he took leave of the younger man 'with a kind of pathetic briskness'—an affecting occasion, movingly described in the great *Life* (B 4. 339). Six months later, on 13 December 1784, Johnson died at his home in Bolt Court, off the north side of Fleet Street. He was buried at Westminster Abbey a week later. A flood of reminiscences appeared over the next few years, headed by the biographies of Hester Thrale, John Hawkins, and Boswell; but the great work was done, and a huge contribution to English letters and to the spirit of the nation had been completed.

3 A world of books

'I was bred a bookseller, and have not forgotten my trade' (L 2. 283).

Several great authors have had a close connection with the book-trade, but Johnson was more deeply embroiled in the business of book production than any writer of his stature. Just how well he understood the economics of bookselling is clear from a letter he wrote in March 1776, which Boswell printed in the *Life* (B 2. 424—6). This incorporates a detailed calculation of the expenses and profits incurred on a typical volume by the publisher, the wholesaler, and the provincial bookseller. Johnson had prolonged firsthand contacts with all three of these groups, and spoke with real authority.

His background in the commercial side of literature began with his early years in his father's bookshop. It continued with his sojourn in Grub Street, and close links with the trade were maintained in the middle of his career as he wrote regularly for the London journals, and produced the *Dictionary* on behalf of leading London booksellers. Throughout his life he remained an 'author by trade or profession', and he knew the splendours and miseries of the calling as intimately as any of the hacks and dunces who figure in literary mythology. Indeed, despite Pope's admiration for Johnson's impressive poetic début in *London*, one cannot help suspecting that if the second book of *The Dunciad* had been written in 1738 instead of 1728, Johnson would have been lucky to escape at least passing allusion among the participants in the contests of poets, novelists, and journalists. In the 1750s he helped to manage the *Literary Magazine*. Then, in the final phase of his career, when Johnson had reached the pinnacle of eminence, he remained sufficiently in touch with the haunts of his youth to produce an unequalled series of portraits of the literary life in his studies of the English poets—again a task which originated as a bookseller's commission. In the summer of 1780 Johnson proposed to Fanny Burney that they should visit together a house demolished in the Gordon Riots. Neither had ever visited the literal Grub Street, on the northern fringes of the City: but both, said Johnson, 'had a very good right to go, so we'll visit the mansions of our progenitors, and take up our own freedom together' (D&L 1. 415). The very language is that of the guild system, the basis of recruitment to the book-trades.

It is worth exploring each of these phases briefly. Michael Johnson's troubled career as a bookseller would have given Samuel, before he had passed through boyhood, a sharp sense of the vicissitudes of one branch, at least, of the book-trade. A more positive effect was produced by the contents of the shop; Johnson had a free run of a large collection of learned literature, especially theology and the classics, designed to tempt the clergy of the diocese of Lichfield. This laid the foundation of the Olympian knowledge he later commanded. Also there were sufficient stocks of 'small books and pleasant histories'—popular chapbooks, almanacs, ballads, and the like—to inspire in the boy a love of chivalric romances which he retained throughout his life. One of the best-known stories told of Johnson's youth concerns his unwillingness to serve on his father's stall at Uttoxeter market; long afterwards, as an elderly man, he once stood there bareheaded in the rain 'for a considerable time', in order to expiate the fault (B 4. 373). The anecdote is generally used to make a point about Johnson's predisposition to feelings of guilt; we ought equally to remind ourselves that it shows an early rejection of books as commercial objects, precisely the conjunction happily adopted by the mature Johnson.

The world of pure, disinterested scholarship—of libraries rather than auction-houses—was largely closed to Johnson after his career at Oxford was aborted and his intended career as a schoolmaster proved a failure. (He did have the opportunity to catalogue the vast Harleian Library, and indeed, as an early biographer, Thomas Tyers, said: 'He would have made an admirable library-keeper' (JM, 2. 361).) Instead he was thrust in the literary and commercial maelstrom of literary London. Crucially, he began to work for the first regular journal devoted to the world of books and newspapers, the *Gentleman's Magazine*. This had been started in 1731, some seven years before Johnson came to work on it; its founder, significantly, was a printer, Edward Cave. Johnson contributed material of various kinds, including short biographies, translations, and reviews. Perhaps the most 'creative' of his tasks was to supply the fictionalized record of parliamentary proceedings at a time when direct reporting was illegal. Cave also published Johnson's *Life of Savage*; the dissolute poet was one of a group of professional writers whom Johnson had come to know during his early days on the staff of the magazine. The biography which emerged, a year after Savage's death in 1743, is one of the classic studies of a creative personality in torment; but its interest lies in social psychology as much as in private pathology. It is far more than a genre study of the calamities of authorship; rather, the book gives us a close account of the ways in which literary talent interacts with a market economy, in which patronage works (or does not work), and in which an 'author to let' (as Savage had himself characterized the job) shapes his career to the needs of society.

The central dialectic of the book involves a contrast between private needs and public demands—Savage's own 'creative' drives, which brought him poverty and social ostracism, set against the requirements for worldly success.

But no sooner had he received his pension, than he withdrew to his darling privacy, from which he returned in a short time to his former distress, and for some part of the year generally lived by chance, eating only when he was invited to the tables of his acquaintances, from which the meanness of his dress often excluded him . . . He lodged as much by accident as he dined and passed the night, sometimes in mean houses, which are set open at night to any casual wanderers, sometimes in cellars among the riot and filth of the meanest and most profligate of the rabble. (LOP 2. 398)

Johnson does not pause to remind us that Savage's intended poetic manuscript was itself entitled *The Wanderer*. The image of the poet is beginning to be defined as that of the self-exiled Byronic figure, a vagrant of the soul: Savage's own seedy life echoes this existential pattern at the level of social existence. Again, there is a contrast between the sordid living conditions and the high intellectual aspirations of the calling:

In this manner passed those days and those nights, which nature had enabled him to have employed in elevated speculations, useful studies, or pleasing conversation. On a bulk, in a cellar, or in a glass-house among thieves and beggars, was to be found the author of the *Wanderer*, the man of exalted sentiments, extensive views and curious observations ...

It is impossible to miss here the sense that Johnson is talking about himself as well as his friend. After all, his own greatest poem was to open with a vision of 'extensive views' (*Vanity of Human Wishes*, ll. 1–2). The prospects denied to Savage are set out in a series of disconsolate optative verbs: 'the man whose remarks on life might have assisted the statesman, whose ideas of virtue might have enlightened the moralist, whose eloquence might have influenced senates, and whose delicacy might have polished courts.' It can be no accident that Johnson, in his early thirties, was defining failure in terms of a frustrated literary career, the kind of thing he had witnessed in the case of his close ally Richard Savage, and which seemed to replicating itself—less dramatically—in his own experience of the writer's life.

Johnson's middle years were dominated by vocational pressures: we know little of his inmost being during these years. In retrospect the period embodies what looks like a success story, though it is evident that this is not how it felt to Johnson at the time. There was the long struggle to complete, with limited help from copyists, the great *Dictionary*, itself a tribute to the corporate initiative and financial stability of the booksellers who grouped together to promote the venture. The need was for what has been called 'a standard and standardizing dictionary'. Like Chambers' *Cyclopaedia*, the *Encyclopaedia Britannica*, and the French *Encyclopédie* (all produced in Johnson's lifetime), the work demonstrates the kind of major undertaking now possible through the developed capitalist resources of the book-trade. Shakespeare or Milton could not and would not have wished to produce a dictionary on this scale; but even if they had, there would not have been the publishing capacity to launch such a massive piece of book-making.

At the same time Johnson was continuing to contribute to the *Gentleman's Magazine*, although his regular editorial stint came to an end in about 1744. He was also writing a good deal for other booksellers, including a variety of journeyman work of the kind

Johnson prided himself on. We know from Joshua Reynolds that he believed there were two things he could do very well: 'one is an introduction to any literary work, stating what it is to contain, and how it should be executed in the most perfect manner; the other is a conclusion, showing from various causes why the execution has not been equal to what the author promised to himself and to the public' (B 1. 292). The immediate outcome was a series of prefaces to the *Gentleman's Magazine* annually, and then numerous dedications and introductions to the works of other men and women. In the long term, there were to be what we generally call the *Lives of the Poets*, but which were originally conceived and published as *Prefaces Biographical and Critical to the Works of the most Eminent English Poets*. This shift of usage conceals the fact that Johnson was again working at the invitation of the booksellers, that is, writing on commission the kind of 'introduction' to each poet which he knew he could perform so well.

It was in this phase, too, that Johnson prepared himself for the task of periodical essayist, undertaken in turn as the *Rambler*, the *Adventurer*, and the *Idler*. These papers appeared at regular intervals, weekly or twice-weekly; the two latter papers came out as parts of journals with miscellaneous contents, rather than as separate essays in their own right. These are the working conditions of the journalist rather than those of the creative artist as we understand that role today. Perhaps no great writer has written more consistently with the printer's devil at his elbow. It is less important, though relevant, that the papers give us many vignettes of the literary life, such as the doings of the would-be critic Dick Mimim in the *Idler*, and sharp insights into what Johnson recognized as an 'age of authors'. Characteristic topics for *Rambler* papers are 'The anxieties of literature not less than those of public stations' and 'An author's treatment from six patrons'. Moreover, Johnson wrote here some of the earliest set discussions of literary criticism (no. 3), the novel (no. 4), and biography (no. 60); it is apt that he, above all others, should have celebrated 'the dignity and usefulness of biography'. He knew that the creating spirit and the everyday living of an individual cannot be precisely equated, but he was always reluctant to split off the writer from his or her work. If our own age has seen, wishfully at least, the

17

death of the author, then Johnson presides over his or her birth, in the sense that he recognizes with special clarity the human impulses which feed into an act of creation, and the social circumstances which both constrain and facilitate that act. It is a lesson which has to be constantly relearnt in eras of rhetorical dogma and formalism, such as the neoclassic and the post-modernist periods.

The last phase is the most familiar portion of Johnson's life, and can be treated more briefly. By far the most significant datum here is the appearance of the *Lives of the Poets*. In most of the key lives—those of Milton, Dryden, Addison, Pope, and Swift, in particular—there is an intricate mental commerce between the inner being of the poet and the external realities of his career in the world. To this day no one has written better of the way in which Pope's letters, published by their author in 1737 after a subterfuge involving the bookseller Curll, reflect his drive for success and his inmost sense of his own being: 'Pope may be said to write always with his reputation in his head' (LOP 3. 160). Formally the biographical and critical sections are separate, but a coherent picture emerges in which neither side totally dominates (there are exceptions; the account of Savage, lifted from its earlier context, remains comparatively thin on literary analysis, whilst the life of Cowley is rightly famous for its pioneering assessment of the metaphysical style, with little more than perfunctory treatment of Cowley the man). Overall, the achievement of the *Lives* is to be found in their vivid recreation of the creative personality. It does not matter in the end whether Johnson is talking about Swift's desperate old age—technically, a biographical issue—or the portrayal of Pandemonium in *Paradise Lost*—technically a critical issue. In both cases Johnson fixes hard on the evidence, adjudicates and discriminates, isolates the emotional as well as the intellectual points at stake, and comes to a clear verdict on the material. Unlike some biographers, he knew that literature is more than a mere expression of personality or the resultant of external experience. Unlike some critics, he knew that books are not created by mental or linguistic structures, but by sentient human beings abroad in the world.

As remarked, Johnson became the subject of a series of biographies soon after his death. These range from instant compilations of little merit to the more profound studies of Hawkins, Hester Piozzi, Boswell, and Arthur Murphy. ('How many maggots have crawled out of that great body!' Burke exclaimed to Hannah More.) However, scarcely any item in this miscellaneous group fails to reveal Johnson as a working writer, and as a man deeply involved in the literary life of his time. Indeed, we owe our sense of the conditions of eighteenth-century authorship more to Boswell than to any other source: he does not tell the full story, but along with the *Life of Savage* and certain *Ramblers* and *Idlers*, the *Life of Johnson* is the most reliable guide to what the rise of professional authorship meant to those involved in the process. Today we take for granted such things as regular reviewing of new books; the production of long series of classic texts; the punctual appearance of standard reference works; and the subsidy of major books in progress by publishers. None of these had existed in any developed way during the previous phases of literature, in England or anywhere else. As we have seen, Johnson's own career brought him into crucial relation with these developments. Despite all the technological and economic changes which have since occurred, this is still in essence the world we inhabit. Johnson wrote great books, but he also took part in the great instauration of modern literature.

4 Ideas and beliefs

Diverse and complex Johnson may be—like anyone of spiritual depth—but certain strands run through every department of his writing. For example, the fear of personal dissolution which pervades his solemn and religious writing turns up in an ostensibly secular guise in the final *Idler* (no. 103) on 'the secret horror of the last'. In literary and moral discussion, as in theology, Johnson was firmly against what he saw as innovation for the sake of it: 'the mental disease of the present generation', he writes in *Rambler* no. 154, 'is impatience of study, contempt of the great masters of ancient wisdom, and a disposition to rely wholly upon unassisted genius and natural sagacity'—a comment that might easily have been applied to a third-rate writer in the *Lives of the Poets*. The same criticism of 'a contempt for all authority' is expressed in one of his sermons (Y 14. 77), this time defined as a theological issue. In linguistic matters Johnson perceived the 'exuberance of signification' (W 10. 49) which words could obtain, and worried about containing this anarchic power; in literary matters he feared the despotic hold of the imagination, whilst recognizing that creativity necessarily meant opening the reader's eyes to experience with some fresh sense of wonder. Just as in ordinary conversation he was able to say 'the most common things in the newest manner', as Thomas Tyers put it (JM 2. 366), so he attempted in his most serious writing to bestow novelty on familiar truths. In religious contexts he tried to show that 'hardness of heart' was an insensitivity to duty and to God's goodness; in political contexts he opposed what he saw as cruelty and indifference to suffering. And so on.

The next four chapters of this book are divided into sections on such topics as religion, politics, society, and history. Yet we retain the sense, as we read Johnson, that the same voice is addressing us on each of these topics: apart from anything else, certain habits of language betray Johnson's consistent purposes. In one of the most searching early numbers of the *Rambler* (no. 7), he writes of the need 'to make the future predominate over the present'. In

Rasselas, Imlac observes that 'there is no man whose imagination does not sometimes predominate over his reason' (Y 16. 150). Finally, in the *Journey to the Western Islands*, comes a clinching case: 'Whatever withdraws us from the power of our senses; whatever makes the past, the distant, or the future, predominate over the present, advances us in the dignity of thinking beings' (Y 9. 148). Spread across works written over a quarter of a century, in very different generic contexts, these usages show Johnson reaching out for a concept of *predominance*, that is, of forcing higher matters to oust lesser. Compare the usage, 'in political relations, good cannot be complete, it can only be predominant' (Y 9. 60); as well as, 'Shakespeare makes nature predominate over accident' (Y 7. 65). We could take other terms which crop up throughout his work, most obviously in key books: the prefaces to the *Dictionary* and the Shakespeare; the periodical essays; *Rasselas*; the *Journey* and the *Lives of the Poets*. We should find not a pure philosophical consistency, but a coherent pattern of usage. Another pervasive motif is the danger of pedantry, by which Johnson understood 'that minute knowledge which is derived from particular sciences and studies in opposition to the general notions supplied by a wide survey of life and nature'.

Religion

Johnson has been called a troubled believer, but the expression is misleading. His doubts concerned not the central tenets of the Christian faith, but rather his own worthiness in professing the faith, and an uncertainty of his own salvation. In fact, his forthright and orthodox Christianity lay at the heart of all he did and wrote. It is, therefore, odd that most general accounts of his work pay no explicit attention to this dimension of his writing. Excellent specialist monographs have been directed towards his religious life, but almost all surveys divide his career into phases relating to a key activity—the journalist, the moralist, the poet, the lexicographer, the critic, and so on. Running through all these separate endeavours, from start to finish, was the core of his creative self—Johnson the religious being.

In middle life, Boswell tells us, Johnson

was offered a living of considerable value in Lincolnshire, if he were inclined to enter holy orders ... But he did not accept of it; partly I believe from a conscientious motive, being persuaded that his temper and habits rendered him unfit for that assiduous and familiar instruction to the vulgar and ignorant which he held to be an essential duty in a clergyman. (B 1. 320)

Both the nature of the offer and the imputed grounds for rejection are significant. It had been thought that Johnson might be ready and able to embark on a new career as a clergyman; the offer came not from a stranger but from Bennet Langton senior, who knew him well. Again, the scruples which may have led Johnson to refuse the offer exemplify his high conception of the clergyman's role, in addition to his profound sense of his own unworthiness. We might feel that he would have made an exceedingly good country parson if he could have brought himself to accept such a charge: the manner in which he invited home an unknown stranger, 'a kind of Methodist, full of texts, but ill-instructed', whom he had seen at church (Y 1. 94), suggests that he had the patience and tolerance to deal with the pastoral tasks to which Boswell referred.

We all know that Johnson did not take the cloth. What he did do, however, was to compose something like forty sermons (B 5. 67), of which twenty-eight survive. These were written for others to deliver. In addition, he wrote a large number of prayers for his own private use. These two categories of material provide the main evidence for us to assess his religious position. Apart from that, we have incidental observations in other writings and spoken comments which were reported by his biographers. It could indeed be argued that the *Rambler* constitutes a series of lay sermons; its concerns overlap those of the true homiletic productions at every point. A final body of evidence is to be found in the large number of works of a religious cast listed in the catalogue of his library. His books included devotional manuals, sermons, church histories, and of course scriptures and scriptural commentaries. In his private meditations, as we shall see, he was constantly adjuring himself to persevere with his readings of the Bible. The fact is simple; the Bible and the Book of Common Prayer were the texts most frequently in his head. His prayers adapt the idiom of the Prayer Book, his meditations echo the cadences of the Psalms. Anyone who wishes to understand Johnson in depth should consult first not a psychoanalyst but a theologian.

The prayers offer the most direct land-line to his inner being. They are full of self-reproaches about a life given him by God and lavished away on 'useless trifles ... [and] vain searches after things which thou hast hidden from me' (Y 1. 48). He constantly regrets the 'time lost in idleness' and the 'vain scruples' which occupy him (Y 1. 70). He sees himself as 'depraved with vain imaginings, and entangled in long habits of Sin' (Y 1. 63). In the accents almost of the Litany, he enjoins his Lord to 'deliver and preserve me from vain terrors' (Y 1. 76). In 1764 he poignantly records, 'I have now spent fifty-five years in resolving, having from the earliest time almost that I can remember been forming schemes of a better life' (Y 1. 81). Among the most famous of these resolutions are repeated statements of intent 'to rise early', as well as to apply himself to study, to drink less strong liquor, to go to church (something he did not do with very great regularity), 'to oppose laziness, by doing what is to be done', to 'reclaim imagination' (probably, to curb sexual fantasies), to keep a daily journal, and to draw up a comprehensive scheme of living. These examples are taken from a single place, the birthday resolutions of 1760 (Y 1. 71), but they could be paralleled at every stage of his life. Johnson believed that he was fighting a losing battle in most instances. It is easy for us with hindsight to dismiss these self-recriminations as pathological, in our knowledge that Johnson lived honourably, produced more good writing in a month than the rest of us would be capable of delivering in a lifetime, and achieved so much that it no longer matters a shred at what time he got up in the morning. This is a crass response. Johnson's tormented self-enquiry was the condition of his greatness; if he had not examined his own life so closely, he would not have commanded such a firm grasp of the fate of humanity at large. Admittedly, there is something comic at first glance about his elaborate table on reading a given number of lines a day (presumably from the Bible); this yields some neat proportional sums—17,280 lines a year, if he read sixty lines a day for six days a week—and comes close to suggesting the calculations of accumulative sins worked out by the Reverend Augustus Toplady, that stern Calvinistic thinker whom Johnson met at a celebrated dinner party given by the Dilly brothers in 1773.

Prayers were composed annually on certain set occasions: the New Year, Easter, Johnson's birthday in September. But the most personal are those he wrote in commemoration of his wife's death, which had taken place on 17 March 1752—after the change in the calendar that year he generally marked the occasion on 28 March. He made a series of resolutions over her coffin, and adverted to these when recalling the event in years to come. There is a heartfelt simplicity in these prayers, in which he 'annually purposed to amend my life' (Y 1. 257). For many years he also fasted on this occasion; once he noted, 'I am this night easier than is customary on this anniversary, but am not sensibly enlightened' (Y 1. 148).

The memory of his wife continued to haunt Johnson for decades to come. Owing to the way in which his papers have been preserved, it is often hard to separate his prayers and meditations from ordinary journal entries for everyday activities. Tetty appears suddenly amidst references to dinner engagements, charities dispersed, and medical data such as bowel movements. In April 1767 he writes, 'On March 28, thought on poor dear Tetty by accident, and designed to reform but forgot it' (Y 1. 113). Three years later he notes:

When I recollect the time in which we lived together, my grief for her departure is not abated, and I have less pleasure in any good that befalls me, because she does not partake it. On many occasions I think what she would have said or done. When I saw the sea at Brighthelmston [Brighton] I wished for her to have seen it with me. (Y 1. 127)

Johnson's spirituality was not a thing apart from the rest of his life. In the same breath he will ask for deliverance from 'needless terrors', resolve to learn Dutch, plan to write a history of his own melancholy, decide to 'avoid all singularity', and note down incidental expenses. He also devoted considerable effort to translating the Prayer Book collects into Latin.

Apart from the prayers, the most moving of his personal records concern his regular acts of charity. The same day as he receives the quarterly instalment of his pension (that is, £75), he promptly lends the improvident bookseller Tom Davies £25 of it (this happens more than once). He gave his friend Joseph Reed a guinea 'to relieve him from the spunging house' (a temporary place of confinement for debtors). As representative as any of the entries are these, for 17/18 March 1765:

17 SUNDAY. Remembered, I think on the heavy day my dear departed wife. Went to church in the afternoon. Came home, recommended Tetty. Resolved or hoped to combat sin and to reform life, but at night drank wine.

MONDAY 18. Eheu! M [bowel movement] 3 in bed this morning with litle difficulty. At 5 p.m. at Trails [Thrales']. Begged a guinea for the widow with four children that sells herbs. Xp [expenses] Fr [ank Barber] 7s., coach 2s., chariot 1s.; in all 10s. (Y 1. 89)

The prayers emerge from this mass of domestic detail as natural extensions of his hourly concerns. The same month, incidentally. Johnson paid back six guineas which he had borrowed to send his dying mother, six years before.

Johnson's sermons are less personal in flavour, but they do indicate his main religious beliefs. Most were written for his lifelong friend John Taylor, a former lawyer and a tireless ecclesiastical place-hunter who ended up with a clutch of preferments, and who performed the service at Johnson's own funeral (H 276). Many commentators have thought it odd that Johnson should have been so close to the worldly and rather boorish Taylor, but he acknowledged to Hester Thrale that Taylor was 'better acquainted with [his] *heart* than any man or woman now alive' (A 70). It was only in 1825 that the sermons were included in a collection of Johnson's works.

Johnson admitted that he found composing sermons relatively easy, and he was ready enough to do it 'for sundry beneficed clergymen', as Sir John Hawkins tells us, at a fee of two guineas a time. His interest in homiletic writing went back a long way, and he was to remind John Wilkes at a famous dinner-party at Dilly's in 1781 that 'sermons make a considerable branch of English literature' (B 4. 105). His models are chiefly traditional—Hooker, Jeremy Taylor, the Restoration divines—and the themes are the familiar ones of pulpit oratory. Johnson warns against the 'pernicious conceit of wisdom', the form of pride most incident to the educated persons he often addresses. He enjoins his listeners to avoid 'hardness of heart', that is, insensitivity to religious claims and duties; he observes that 'sorrow and fear and anxiety are . . . adjuncts of repentance' (see Sermon 2). Characteristically, he warns against 'an overfondness for novelty' (Y 14. 78), a fault which, as we shall see, ran through most branches of thought in Johnson's estimation.

Johnson was in most doctrinal respects an orthodox Anglican of his time. This is despite an unusually eclectic range of influences. After his irreligious teenage years, he was greatly affected by reading at Oxford William Law's celebrated book, *A Serious Call to a Devout and Holy Life* (1728), then hot from the press, which turned Johnson towards religious issues. In particular, Law expounded the ill effect of the passions on our conduct, and saw pride as the root of most backslidings from virtue, as far as the would-be devout were concerned. Moreover, he identified sloth as a particular obstacle to the good life—a circumstance Johnson understood all too well. Another strong influence which has been detected was that of the Arian and near-deistic thinker Samuel Clarke, a man widely distrusted by orthodox churchmen; Johnson seems to have admired the clear rationality of Clarke's approach to religious questions, and his warnings against undue scrupulosity. But much of Johnson's theology is of a more traditional cast, deriving from the Church Fathers and from the great Protestant preachers of the sixteenth and seventeenth centuries. (His revisions for the fourth edition of the *Dictionary* (1773) suggest renewed acquaintance with this body of writing.) Some commentators have seen increased liberalism in Johnson's thought as time went on, especially in regard to Roman Catholicism and dissent, but at Oxford in the very last summer of his life he acknowledged that he would not quit the faith in which he had been reared: 'I would be a papist if I could. I have fear enough; but an obstinate rationality prevents me. I shall never be a papist, unless on the near approach of death, of which I have a very great terror' (B 4. 289).

In fact it has been suspected that Johnson did go through some kind of deathbed apostasy, mainly on the basis of his very last prayer, composed a week before his death, which refers to 'my late conversion' (Y 1. 417–18). Some people, including the poet Cowper, believed that Johnson had undergone conversion to an

Evangelical faith, but it is now generally accepted that the phrase means his belated submission to God's will, and his repentance, rather than acceptance of any new creed. However, we cannot be absolutely certain what went on in Johnson's last days, despite prolonged investigation of this matter; his very real fear of death conditioned all his good resolves. He found neither holy living nor holy dying easy. But then his concept of these was more demanding than the one which satisfies many of us. The most he could tell Hawkins was that he was 'almost' persuaded that he was 'in the state of reconciliation with God' (H 270).

It could be argued that terror of divine punishment in the life to come was an orthodox incentive to repentance among the devout. Still, Johnson's acknowledged fears at the prospect of death astonished Hawkins, who tried to soothe him by pointing to the 'uniform course of virtue' which his life had displayed (H 245); but to no avail. Johnson refused to accept any consolatory advice, however well meant, which implied any certainty of salvation. Equally, it was still entirely routine Anglican belief—despite the well-known advance of 'benevolent' philosophy—to hold that humanity was blighted by original sin, which only total submission to the divine will could obviate. But Johnson's acceptance of the dogma has its own peculiar note of fierceness, as when he told Lady McLeod on Skye that man was no more naturally good than a wolf is (B 5. 211). We can attempt to deflect some of these seemingly obsessive concerns into the domain of traditional theology, but we shall never altogether lose sight of a residuum of intense personal suffering. It is sad that such an innately good man, with all his multifarious good deeds and silent acts of charity, could not have been happier. Yet there is another sense in which he became a deeper and richer person because of his acute awareness of the perils of mortal existence. 'Perhaps', wrote Thomas Tyers, 'Johnson had more of life, by his intenseness of living . . . He was all his life preparing himself for death' (JM 2. 336). To contemplate his lonely struggle with despair, as registered in the prayers he wrote, is to come close to his strength as well as his weakness. Guilt and a sense of worthlessness served to inhibit personal fulfilment, but at the same time they drove him to work and they inspired his generous and giving way of life.

27

The war on paradox

> It is sometimes necessary to repeat what we all know.
> All mapmakers should place the Mississippi in the
> same location, and avoid originality. It may be boring,
> but one has to know where he is. We cannot have the
> Mississippi flowing toward the Rockies for a change.
>
> Saul Bellow, *Mr Sammler's Planet*

In the moral sphere, Johnson was a campaigner on behalf of
orthodoxy. This has been an ungrateful role in the twentieth
century, as figures as different as Evelyn Waugh and C. S. Lewis
have discovered. The Romantic movement ushered in a view that
originality is the supreme virtue, and triteness the deadliest of
vices. Since the time of Baudelaire and Flaubert, every would-be
writer has shunned the commonplaces of bourgeois conformity.
Hippolyte Taine's wonderfully paradoxical statement ('his truths
are too true') illustrates the very habit of mind against which
Johnson directed much of his fire. 'When speculation has done its
worst', he writes in *Idler* no. 36, 'two and two still make four.'
This is asserted in the course of defending a favourite Johnsonian
theme, namely that 'the great differences that disturb the peace of
mankind are not about ends, but means'. As so often, there is a
direct analogue in the *Life of Johnson* to the *Idler* reference: this
is when he upbraids an inaccurate writer, William Tasker: 'Sir,
you are giving a reason for it, but that will not make it right. You
may have a reason why two and two should make five; but they
will still make but four' (B 3. 375). Like Bellow's narrator, Johnson
emphasizes the need to preserve certain inviolable certainties:
much was speculative in the map-making of America in the
eighteenth century, but even then it was well known that the
Mississippi flowed south to the Gulf of Mexico.

Of course, Johnson being Johnson, he was not interested in
reasserting tame platitudes for the sake of it. As Peter Levi has
well observed: 'To make common sense sound unpredictable is
one of his weapons.' Much of the energy which comes through
when Johnson addresses moral topics, either in his literary works
or in his conversation, derives from the effort to give familiar
ideas the force of novelty or surprise. Johnson clearly realized that
hereditary truths had no prescriptive right to our assent. In

discussing the rules of drama in *Rambler* no. 156, he insists that 'it ought to be the first endeavour of a writer to distinguish nature from custom; or that which is established because it is right, from that which is right only because it is established'. He took a similar view of moral injunctions. The need was to uncover the underlying principles governing moral life, and then to reassert these in challenging and effective ways. 'The task of the author', *Rambler* no. 3 opens, 'is, either to teach what is not known, or to recommend known truths by his manner of adorning them.' This adornment takes various forms, but it always results in trenchant restatement of ideas that have been too easily accepted. 'The common maxims of life' receive Johnson's assent only after an active process of testing and examination. In the account of Swift's style in the *Lives of the Poets*, Johnson comments on the virtues and limitations of a bare manner of writing: 'For purposes merely didactic, when something is to be told that was not known before, it is the best mode, but against that inattention by which known truths are suffered to lie neglected it makes no provision; it instructs, but it does not persuade' (LOP 3. 52). Persuasion is a central part of the authorial function, as practised by Johnson, and such an undertaking calls for means of adorning the unvarnished truth so as to remind readers of what they have conveniently forgotten.

'It is not sufficiently considered', Johnson wrote in the *Rambler*, 'that men more frequently require to be reminded than informed.' Similarly, in the sphere of religion, we are told that 'the great art of piety ... is the perpetual renovation of the motives to virtue'—this was indeed the reason for establishing rites and liturgies (*Rambler* no. 7). Given the perpetual use of verbs such as 'remind', 'renovate', 'recall', 'recommend', it follows that the business of the moralist is to infuse fresh vigour into propositions which otherwise would fail to incite virtue because of their depleted strength. But this had to be done without falling into the specious form of novelty which is found in paradox, since it was precisely the straightforward and un-oblique truth which needed to be conveyed. Common experience is the bedrock of Johnson's ethical teaching, and indeed his entire moral outlook is predicated on the crucial value to be placed on the most familiar aspects of daily living—again a situation quite opposed to the teaching of many modern thinkers, who have emphasized moments of epiphany or experiences of defamiliarizing novelty.

Johnson has his own form of unmasking and demythologizing, but it consists usually of revealing unsuspected richness in apparently commonplace areas of life. He inhabits a universe where the commonplace reflects abiding truth. In *Adventurer* no. 108 he writes of 'certain topics which never are exhausted', and of 'images and sentiments' which perpetually elicit assent and pleasure in the mind of man. Many moral sentiments, we are told, are perfectly 'adapted to our state' and so they always receive approbation. Such is the comparison of the life of man with the duration of a flower, 'a thought which, perhaps, every nation has heard warbled in its own language . . . yet this comparison must always please, because every heart feels its justness, and every hour confirms it by example'. Similarly, there is the precept which 'directs us to use the present hour'. This, says Johnson, 'every moralist may venture to inculcate, because it will always be approved, and because it is always forgotten' (Y 2. 447). Today we might easily misread this as irony. But the message in Johnson is not that moralists can safely go on repeating these (true but trite) platitudes, because no one is listening. It is that moralists should be encouraged to state them again, because we are otherwise prone to neglect these essential truths.

Clearly, we are not far here from some of Johnson's critical pronouncements. We think immediately of the commendation of Gray's *Elegy*, that it 'abounds with images which find a mirror in every mind, and with sentiments to which every bosom returns an echo'. As a result of this quality in the poem, Johnson is able proudly 'to concur with the common reader' (LOP 3. 441). Moving in a slightly different direction, we could pick up a phrase from the Preface to the *Dictionary*, which refers to 'the diction of common life' as exemplified in the language of Shakespeare: if this were extracted from the plays, Johnson tells us, 'few ideas would be lost to mankind, for want of English words, in which they might be expressed' (W 10. 53). The linguistic implications of this statement are best considered in another chapter (pp. 62–5 below). What matters here is that Johnson scrutinized the most ordinary levels of 'common colloquial language' in Shakespeare, and did not identify Shakespeare's verbal power with his ability to think up 'multitudinous seas incarnadine'. We may recall here Hester Piozzi's comment on Johnson's own allegedly pompous language: she remarked that, though he had been accused of using 'big words', he did so 'only when little ones would not express his meaning as clearly' (A 158). It is with words as with ideas at large: one begins from the common stock, and has recourse to the more recondite items only in case of particular need. Shakespeare is indeed the poet of nature partly because his language incorporates a constant buzz of allusion to the familiar, the domestic, and the banal—everything that was to be handed over in the nineteenth century to dullards like Bouvard and Pécuchet.

Another inference we can draw from this evidence is that Johnson's hostility to many of the new ideas abroad in his time derived from the tendency to paradox they involved. In the very first summer of Boswell's acquaintance with Johnson, he reported a conversation on the 'fashionable topic' of Rousseau's views on civilization: at one point Johnson asserts, 'Rousseau, and all those who deal in paradoxes, are led away by a childish desire of novelty' (B 1. 441). To be sure, Johnson understood the appeal of novelty, and the need to keep on refreshing familiar truths with the spice of vivid restatement. He probably thought that Rousseau had produced too specialized an anthropology, laying too much weight on exceptional cases and avoiding the humdrum realities of most people's lives: it was a settled conviction that 'the true state of every nation is the state of common life' (Y 9. 22), a fact one would more easily glean from the careful description and analysis of the Highlands than from the hectic theorizing of Rousseau, in which the philosopher speculated on savage peoples he had never visited. What Johnson called 'cant' is often not just insincerity but also untested experience, and that becomes the natural outlet for a paradoxical vein of thinking. Writers like Hume sophisticated relatively straightforward moral choices by inventing layer upon layer of scruples; but 'no man need stay to be virtuous till the moralists have determined the essence of virtue; our duty is made apparent by its proximate consequences' (*Idler* no. 37). In turn Boswell inherited these views on the fashionable theories regarding the savage and civilized state of man, and in his paper *The Hypochondriack*, no. 20 (1779) Boswell opposed the 'ingenious speculations' of Rousseau and Lord

31

Monboddo: 'For me, who love comfort a great deal better than paradox . . . I cannot be of opinion that a man who lies in the open air, or at best in a wretched hut, is happier than a man who has a good warm convenient house.' The accents are not precisely Johnsonian, but the sentiments are.

It is no accident that the spokesman for the era which dawned as Johnson came to the end of his life was William Blake, for whom paradox enshrined a whole metaphysic and a whole cosmology. Many of his most graphic statements are couched in terms of oxymoron ('The road of excess leads to the palace of wisdom'—one of the 'Proverbs of Hell' that deliberately stand orthodox opinion on its head). We are equally unsurprised to find that Blake stood out against Johnson's aesthetic principles ('all sublimity is founded on minute discrimination'), and assailed the *Discourses* of Joshua Reynolds, the friend and literary acolyte of Johnson. Indeed, Blake wrote some scabrous and obscene lines on Johnson in his *Island in the Moon*, composed around the date of Johnson's death. For his part, Johnson would not have wished to be of the Devil's party, even if it meant in Blake's peculiar reasoning that this would have ensured that he was a true poet. Paradox is the necessary instrument of Blake's thought because he wishes to undermine the traditional operation of logical and rational faculties. He values human beings as they transcend the given and aspire to Promethean victories of spirit over matter. Appearances are always deceptive; sub-texts tell the true story, not the literal text; finally, if one pursues these views to their ultimate (as Blake does), sanity is folly, and what the world calls madness is the truest wisdom. It scarcely needs explaining why a similar rhetoric of violent paradox would have been inappropriate to the needs of Johnson, who believed that reason, supported by memory, permitted human beings to make sense of their past lives and regulate their future conduct: 'Judgement and ratiocination suppose something already known, and draw their decisions only from experience' (*Idler* no. 44). To abandon accumulated experience, or to rely on intuition and inspired guesswork, was to go beyond paradox into desperate frenzy.

We must not attempt to force all Johnson's moral views into a pattern of complete uniformity. He knew as well as anyone who has ever lived the complexity of experience, since he above all based his outlook on the mass of empirical evidence, rather than abstract propositions. There are times in his conversation when he appears to be supporting what we might regard as paradox, although more commonly he detects paradox in the speeches of his antagonists. But if he did not achieve, or aim for, perfect consistency, it can at least be claimed that he would have been reluctant to assert blandly: 'Do I contradict myself? Very well then I contradict myself.' In every branch of thought, Johnson stuck to the notion that it was more important to be right than to be provocative or original. 'The basis of all excellence is truth', he wrote in the life of Cowley (LOP 1. 6); a corollary was that to recommend deep religious truths 'by tropes and figures is to magnify by a concave mirror the sidereal hemisphere' (LOP 1. 292). In theological terms, a similar insight is expressed in one of the sermons: 'We cannot make truth, it is our business only to find it' (Y 14. 223). From a modern perspective this could be seen as a tame and quietist position; but in Johnson's mental economy the struggle is no less arduous, even though it involves not so much personal construction of a creed to live by as laborious discovery of an objective order of things, passed down to us across the centuries. To go searching after facile paradoxes is merely to strain to be different for the sake of it:

Hume, and other sceptical innovators, are vain men, and will gratify themselves at any expense. Truth will not afford sufficient food to their vanity; so they have betaken themselves to error. Truth, Sir, is a cow that will yield such people no more milk, and so they are gone to milk the bull. If I could have allowed myself to gratify my vanity at the expense of truth, what fame might I have acquired. (B 1. 444)

An ethic of gradualism

In his concern with 'the common business of the world' (*Rambler* no. 137) and 'the business of common life' (*Rambler* no. 161), Johnson the moralist naturally fixes on certain pervasive attributes of existence, shared by people of every nation, age, and class. One of his most pervasive themes is the need to persevere in our moral life, since what might be impossible as an immediate target may be realizable by dint of repeated small efforts. Indeed, the most characteristic part of Johnson's ethical thought is that concerned with the day-to-day attrition of the examined life, and the consequent need to look for small gains rather than sudden triumphs in appraising our conduct.

This sense of a gradual improvement rather than a once-for-all conversion can be related to other branches of Johnson's thought. It accords with a fundamentally rational version of Christianity, in which abrupt spiritual insights are less to be expected than the benefits of steady application to the habits of prayer and worship. It equally accords with his view of the life of scholarship: in the words of *Rambler* no. 137: 'The chief art of learning, as Locke has observed, is to attempt but little at a time. The widest excursions of the mind are made by short flights frequently repeated; the most lofty fabrics of science are formed by the continued accumulation of single propositions.' Such a life by way of moral accumulation is justified by the fact that 'life consists not of a series of illustrious actions or elegant enjoyments', but rather in 'compliance with necessities, in the performance of daily duties, in the removal of small inconveniencies, in the procurement of petty pleasures' (Y 9. 22)—and here the word 'petty' has no scornful ring. In all departments of living, Johnson sees the need to make a gradual ascent, starting from limited objectives and almost invisible steps upward.

It is on this base that Johnson erects what could again seem a tamely quietist philosophy, but one which is redeemed by the dignity of the labour it involves. If it is true that 'the cure for the greatest part of human miseries is not radical, but palliative' (*Rambler* no. 32), then honour as well as social benefit accrues from any small victories we can attain. A life of struggle can also be a life of limited advancement: 'What remains, but to acquiesce with silence, as in the other insurmountable distresses of humanity? It remains that we retard what we cannot repel, that we palliate what we cannot cure' (Preface to the *Dictionary* (W 10. 64)). Mankind inches forward in the hope of something better. 'The quality of looking forward into futurity seems the unavoidable condition of a being, whose motions are gradual, and whose life is progressive' (*Rambler* no. 2). This last is of course far from a 'progressive' view, in its opposition to a revolutionary or millenarian idea of human nature; it is, however, in many ways an Enlightenment view, based as it is on the sense of man's improvable (if not perfectible) state. It is true that Johnson has the strong inherited sense of what is not possible to limited mortals, 'placed on this isthmus of a middle state'; his work is full of the awareness expressed by Nekayah in *Rasselas*, when she states that 'he does nothing who endeavours to do more than is allowed to humanity' (Y 16. 110). But this does not rule out, indeed it lends greater importance to, achieving the goals which are available to a being only a little lower than the angels. There is such a thing as progress, although it is conceived in a more pragmatic and far less dramatic way than would appeal to revolutionaries. Once, indeed, progress is defined in (quite explicitly) literalist terms: 'The lexicographer at last finds the conclusion of his alphabet' (*Rambler* no. 111).

This is a bitter little private joke, stimulated by the author's slow progress on his own mammoth task at this juncture. But it enforces a general truth. As Johnson sees it, one must divide large phenomena up into component parts and deal with these more convenient units—a basically Lockeian procedure. He observes that human felicity 'is made up of many ingredients, each of which may be shown to be very insignificant' (B 1. 440). Again, in his review of a life of the King of Prussia (1756), Johnson divides up character into constituent parts: 'In every great performance, perhaps in every great character, part is the gift of nature, part the contribution of accident, and part, very often not the greatest part, the effect of voluntary election, and regular design' (W 9. 235). A thinking being will divide up moral experience, as any other, and give priority to the most important element. The lexicographer will finally reach the letter Z, and the moral agent will move through the conquest of minor difficulties to an enhanced capacity to live a worthwhile life.

Early in 1778 Hester Thrale wrote in her journal of Johnson, 'who thinks the vacuity of life the source of all the passions' (T 1. 254). Vacuity could range from existential isolation down to literal solitude: Johnson flippantly told his hostess at Streatham, as an excuse for late rising, that he 'did not like to come down to vacuity'. At the serious end, this reflects his besetting fear of isolation and his need to be spurred into action by the stimulus of others; 'Company is in itself better than solitude and pleasure better than indolence', he told Mrs Thrale (L 2. 50). As he once

35

wrote to Boswell: 'Whatever philosophy [science] may determine of material nature, it is certainly true of intellectual nature, that it *abhors a vacuum*: our minds cannot be empty' (L 1. 254). In the face of 'the incessant cravings of vacancy' (L 1. 191), it is important to exercise the mind, which otherwise '*stagnates* for want of employment'.

Underlying this stress on action is no mere encouragement of busyness for the sake of keeping busy. It is important to cultivate good mental *habits*—'To have the management of the mind is a great art, and it may be attained in a considerable degree by experience and habitual exercise' (B 2. 440). More than that, moral life was a dynamic process and involved constant growth if anything of value was to be achieved. One explicit statement of this view comes in a letter to Mrs Thrale, written a year before Johnson died, in which he comments on her daughter's illness and recovery (advising the girl, characteristically, to 'go back to her arithmetic again'): 'Life to be worthy of a rational being must be always in progression; we must always purpose to do more or better than in time past. The mind is enlarged and elevated by mere purposes, though they end as they begin by airy contemplation' (L 3. 109). Sophia Thrale was to acquire good mental habits, and that meant the slow process of self-improvement, one step at a time, which constitutes human advancement in Johnson's eyes. 'Life is made up', he would say, 'of little things; and that character is the best which does little but repeated acts of beneficence' (A 90). 'Heroic virtues' were not required.

Part of the reason for this emphasis on gradual self-improvement is Johnson's recognition that it is fatally easy to set oneself absurdly big targets and, after the inevitable failure to achieve them, to do nothing. This is the theme of one of his most personally flavoured essays, *Rambler* no. 134. Near the end of the essay the author reaches the typically Johnsonian position: 'He that has abilities to conceive perfection, will not easily be content without it; and, since perfection cannot be reached, will lose the opportunity of doing well in the vain hope of unattainable excellence.' We have come to this point via a meditation on the lure of postponing essential acts, a condition to which Johnson was always subject—as his prayers reveal. He writes here of 'the folly of allowing ourselves to delay what we know cannot finally be escaped', and of 'life languished away in the gloom of anxiety'. The autobiographical note is unmistakable, particularly when we reflect that in 1751, when these words were written, Johnson was on the verge of a prolonged period of depression. He goes on: 'To act is far easier than to suffer; yet we every day see the progress of life retarded by the *vis inertiae*, the mere repugnance to motion, and find multitudes repining at the want of that which nothing but idleness hinders them from enjoying.' He even calls up the almost comic image of Tantalus, groping out towards unreachable fruits: 'but what tenderness can be claimed by those who, though perhaps they suffer the pains of Tantalus, will never lift their hands for their own relief?' Asserting with grim self-reference that 'idleness never can secure tranquillity', Johnson proceeds to anatomize the various causes of inactivity, giving instances rather like those found in the case-histories of self-deception in *Rasselas*: 'he that resolves to unite all the beauties of situation in a new purchase, must waste his life in roving to no purpose from province to province. He that hopes in the same house to obtain every convenience, may draw plans and study Palladio, but will never lay a stone.' The answer to such inertia is to force oneself into action, however trivial or apparently pointless. Harshly, Johnson wrote to Mrs Thrale that 'grief is a species of idleness' (L 1. 313), and he was prone to regard even well-intentioned inactivity as being on the same level as stupid torpor.

So we have an ethic of energetic combat against despair and lethargy. 'Patience and submission are very carefully to be distinguished from cowardice and indolence. We are not to repine, but we may lawfully struggle' (*Rambler* no. 32). Furthermore, 'the safe and general antidote against sorrow is employment... [Sorrow] is remedied by exercise and motion' (*Rambler* no. 47). The antidote could be taken in small doses. It is perhaps for this reason that Johnson so often recommended his friends to study arithmetic: it concentrated the mind wonderfully, and 'prevented his mind from preying upon itself' (B 1. 72). According to Hester Piozzi: 'When Mr Johnson felt his mind...disordered, his constant recurrence was to the study of arithmetic; and one day... he showed me a calculation which I could scarce be made to understand, so vast was the plan of it, and so intricate were the figures' (A 86–7: the subject was converting the national debt into silver bullion). He told Sophia Thrale that 'nothing amuses more harmlessly than computation' (L 3. 54). The only book he took with him to the Highlands was a copy of Cocker's *Arithmetic*, which he gave away on the journey. Boswell adds that 'he was very fond of the precision which calculation produces' (B 2. 289), and this was a further benefit of such study; perhaps the best example occurs in an exchange with Boswell, which demonstrates in a short space Johnson's vein of clear-headed positivism:

BOSWELL. 'Sir Alexander Dick tells me, that he remembers having a thousand people in a year to dine at his house: that is, reckoning each person as one, each time that he dined there.' JOHNSON. 'That, Sir, is about three a day.' BOSWELL. 'How your statement lessens the idea.' JOHNSON. 'That, Sir, is the good of counting. It brings every thing to a certainty, which before floated in the mind indefinitely.' (B 4. 204)

But more commonly, arithmetic (occasionally algebra) is valued as a means of conquering idle or wandering thoughts.

The choice of life

Two of Johnson's outstanding works, *The Vanity of Human Wishes* and *Rasselas*, deal with what the latter calls 'the choice of life'. Their central concern lies with the nature of moral life, involving questions of hope and fulfilment, freedom and necessity, desire and despair. Nowadays we should expect a writer to treat these as broad existential phenomena; Johnson sees them as directly ethical and religious issues.

The Vanity of Human Wishes (1749) is an imitation of Juvenal's tenth satire. Johnson had an intermediate presence in his mind, that is, the translation of this poem by Dryden published in 1693. Johnson uses the same verse form, the heroic couplet, and though his style is a little more grave and formal than Dryden's it remains in the mainline Augustan mode of clear syntax and orderly expression. The central themes are announced early, in lines balancing naked abstractions against familiar metaphors of moral experience:

> Then say how hope and fear, desire and hate,
> O'erspread with snares the clouded maze of fate,

> Where wavering man, betrayed by venturous pride,
> To tread the dreary paths without a guide,
> As treacherous phantoms in the mist delude,
> Shuns fancied ills, or chases airy good.
>
> (ll. 5–10)

The exploration of this 'maze' which ensues adopts a moral vocabulary close to that of the *Rambler*, which appeared in the years immediately following the publication of this poem. Just as *Rambler* no. 6 discusses 'the folly of human wishes and pursuits', so the poem deals in turn with the illusory prospects held out by ambition, whether the lust for military glory or the dream of renown as a scholar. The mood is chiefly sombre, but Johnson did not forget that it was a satire by Juvenal which provided his model, and the celebration of the 'laughing philospher' Democritus, with his 'cheerful wisdom and instructive mirth' (l. 50), should alert us to a vein of rueful contemplation of human inanity. This submerged comedy is often sardonic and bitter, but never cruel. Johnson deals compassionately with the sad trophies of war, where Swift, in *The Conduct of the Allies*, had made a harsh jest of the same topic:

> And mortgaged states their grandsires' wreaths regret,
> From age to age in everlasting debt;
> Wreaths which at last the dear-bought right convey
> To rust on medals, or on stones decay.
>
> (ll. 187–90)

The last line takes the form of chiasmus, a favourite Augustan device; Pope would have augmented the syntactical balance with some phonetic aid (assonance or internal rhyme), but Johnson chooses to make the rhetorical contrast more subdued.

Principally, Johnson conceives of his material in historical terms. The main set-pieces of the poem are character-sketches of prominent figures from the past: the distant past of Xerxes, the middle distance of Wolsey and Laud, the recent past of Charles XII of Sweden and the Elector of Bavaria (who had only recently died when Johnson wrote, although he had been condemned to obscurity after failures in the War of the Austrian Succession). One verse paragraph links the fate of ancient Croesus ('Lydia's monarch') with that of two men who had died in Johnson's own forty-year lifespan, each a great man in his walk but each, in the poet's estimate, flawed and ultimately tragic:

> From Marlborough's eyes the streams of dotage flow,
> And Swift expires a driveller and a show.
>
> (ll. 317–18)

The poem also confronts the destiny of entire nations, suggesting that these triumphant hordes will have their own final collapse, even though for a time the honours they hold before individuals are a powerful bribe:

> For such the steady Romans shook the world;
> For such in distant lands the Britons shine,
> And stain with blood the Danube or the Rhine.
>
> (ll. 180–2)

Johnson is remembering here the noble peroration of Pope's *Windsor Forest*, with its joyous glimpse of the prospects of peace:

> No more my sons shall dye with British blood
> Red Iber's sands, or Ister's foaming flood...

Most forms of ambition are seen as corrupt, and Johnson rejects the easy consolation that at least the would-be scholar in his lonely cell beneath 'Bodley's dome' does no harm to anyone except himself. Reduced by indolence and melancholy to a career marked by 'Toil, envy, want, the patron and the gaol' (l. 160), the student incurs merely personal disappointment. But if the love of fame (a key idea Johnson had borrowed from his friend Edward Young) extends to the search for political power or military conquest, then the lives of many others will be blighted. This is not a distinction Johnson chooses to draw. In either instance, the delusive quality of human aspiration, unguided by the promptings of religious belief, is exemplified, but Johnson's ethical calculations are never too neat to leave human consequence out of the equation.

In its last paragraph the poem moves from its pagan roots towards Christian affirmation, rejecting in the process the supine creed of Stoicism—as it seemed to the author—with its feeble consolations and its refusal to grapple actively with the calamities of life ('Must dull Suspense corrupt the stagnant mind?'). As always, Johnson prefers valiant defeat to passive resignation. In any case, we should not be surprised that orthodox religion takes over at the end, since the very title of the poem has strong echoes of the prophetic books of the Bible. 'Vanity of vanities, saith the preacher...all is vanity' (Ecclesiastes 1: 2). Not quite all, in Johnson's version, since a kind of serenity is achieved in the closing lines, not by ignoring pain or denying the reality of death in some impassive Stoical way, but by grappling with fate and trusting to the wisdom of the Almighty.

Johnson originally intended to give *Rasselas* the title, 'The Choice of Life'. Though he rescinded this decision, the story carries on the work of *The Vanity of Human Wishes* in anatomizing the mistaken paths human beings take when they subject their moral life to unreal or inappropriate systems and guide-lines. The opening metaphor in the poem was that of the maze; in this case, the underlying image is that of a journey in quest for the great good place, prompted by a desire to escape from the valley where the story begins.

The opening sentence of the book suggests that we are to expect a saga of disillusionment: 'Ye who listen with credulity to the whispers of fancy, and pursue with eagerness the phantoms of hope; who expect that age will perform the promise of youth, and that the deficiencies of the present day will be supplied by the morrow; attend to the history of Rasselas prince of Abyssinia' (Y 16. 7). In fact, the work as it develops conveys a certain buoyancy or resilience, and the spoilt ideals which are at first a subject of easy dismissal grow more worthy of serious attention. As the phrasing of the opening sentence may indicate, the dialectic is constructed around a set of ironic oppositions, between promise and performance, hope and actuality. One could of course describe these as 'paradoxes', but it is important to note that they are not desirable states of contrariety, but more like Hegelian antitheses in need of resolution. For Johnson, irony is generally a means towards a more positive end; and whilst *Rasselas* exposes the gap between human aspirations and achievements, it does so in order to urge us towards more suitable and more human goals in life.

We start then, with a Utopia which seems to the young prince and princess a prison; or a paradise with no exits. It is a world of 'pleasure and repose', where discord has been banished. But

Rasselas turns towards 'solitary walks and silent meditation', an emblem in Johnson's work for vain self-regard. He casts aside luxury, forgets 'to taste the dainties that were set before him', and retires 'beyond the sound of music' (Y 16. 12). The third chapter is entitled 'The Wants of Him that Wants Nothing'. Whilst still pondering escape from this apparent felicity, he encounters the first of a series of deluded projectors who fill the narrative. This is the would-be aeronaut, whose flight into the empyrean turns out to be a rapid descent into a lake. Then the prince comes on his mentor, the poet Imlac, who states that the history of a scholarly man 'will not be long', since such a figure is 'neither known or valued' in the world. But Imlac's life-history is allowed five chapters, the fullest biography accorded to any character, and his influence pervades the work from this point on. Ultimately a means of egress is found, and the prince, his sister Nekayah, and Imlac are able to defect from the Happy Valley. The two young people are transported with joy at this prospect: Imlac, who has seen it all before, departs with much more qualified expectations of the world outside.

The travellers reach Cairo, and their education begins. Rasselas has high hopes of the confident young men who give themselves up to a round of pleasure, but he finds their way of life empty and discreditable. He takes up with a cheerful Stoic philosopher, only to return shortly afterwards to find the sage broken by grief at the loss of his daughter, his easy Leibnizian theories about sorrow proving shallow when put to the test of experience. (It is worth recalling here that *Rasselas* appeared within a few months of Voltaire's *Candide*, another philosophic *conte* in which easy answers to the pain of living are summarily derided.) The party next enjoy 'a glimpse of pastoral life', in which they look for the 'innocence and quiet' long attributed to simple Arcadian rustics; but the shepherds show themselves as 'rude and ignorant', overworked, envious, and brutalized by their harsh existence. Similarly, a man of great wealth proves to be under threat from his enemies, so that he has to maintain a permanent guard and to dispatch his treasures abroad. A hermit finds his solitude irksome, and his removal from the world productive only of 'a thousand perplexities of doubt, and vanities of the imagination'. He has indeed already determined to return to the converse of society, since 'the life of a solitary man will be certainly miserable, but not certainly devout' (Y 16. 83). A natural philosopher, perhaps modelled on Samuel Clarke, spouts Deistic platitudes about living in harmony with the fitness of things, but Rasselas 'soon found that this was one of the sages whom he should understand less as he heard him longer'.

So the survey of plans for happiness continues, each episode demonstrating that a quest for the absolute which is not regulated by religious piety or human decency will end in absurdity and ignominy. The prince enquires into people of high station, and finds their existence hopelessly insecure as one rival for power exterminates another. Nekayah explores private life, to discover that families which should promote mutual support are riven by tensions and jealousies. But it is impossible to opt out of this emotional jungle by remaining single—in the famous phrase: 'Marriage has many pains, but celibacy has no pleasures' (Y 16. 99). Every scheme for personal happiness seems to be blocked. Nor do the great cultural monuments of the world possess the lasting value which has been attributed to them. Hence, when the party visit the Pyramids, deemed 'the greatest work of man, except the wall of China', they see that the entire building operation was wasteful, purposeless, and unmeaning. In Imlac's words, 'it seems to have been erected only in compliance with that hunger of imagination which preys upon life, and must always be appeased by some employment' (Y 16. 118). The mighty structure is simply 'a monument of the insufficiency of human enjoyments'. After a melodramatic digression involving the kidnapping of Nekayah's companion, the travellers make their way back to Cairo.

In the climactic episode they are introduced to a distinguished astronomer, who is then exposed as the wildest of all the paranoid self-deceivers who stalk through the book. He is convinced that as a result of his studies he has gained total mastery over the elements, with the power to control weather. He has now grown anxious at the scale of his dominion over nature, and confides in Imlac, ostensibly to name the poet as his successor—though also, one suspects, to share the terrible isolating knowledge he thinks that he possesses. Rasselas and Nekayah are recruited to lead the deluded man back into the sphere of reason. Typically for

43

Johnson, therapy takes the form of inveigling him into ordinary human contacts. The astronomer 'began gradually to delight in sublunary pleasures' (Y 16. 160), and finally the grip of his monomania starts to loosen. A hint of regret perhaps slips through, that he should have to renounce his dreams.

There is time for a visit to the catacombs, and then we abruptly reach 'the conclusion in which nothing is concluded'. Not really so; for the irresolute ambitions of Rasselas and his party have at least been stripped down to sensible proportions. They decide in the closing paragraph of the book to return to Abyssinia. We do not follow them there, since there is no sense that the Happy Valley will now be recognized as the pure Utopia they had failed to identify at the start. On their quest, they have learned to be critical and sceptical of any universal nostrum for human happiness, and they have discovered that there is no uniquely favoured great good place protected from the realities of mortal existence. But their retreat is far from a sign of total defeat. The lesson is, not to quench the unappeasable hunger of the imagination, for Johnson knows that we shall go on longing, but to moderate our expectations of what is possible in the limited order of existence vouchsafed to ordinary human beings. That way we can make a little advance. It is better, Johnson suggests, to settle for minor victories over the destructive forces assailing mankind than to reach out for some supernal order of experience transcending the commonplace virtues of duty, loyalty, humility, and trust. The Promethean quest will end with a belly-flop into the lake. No wonder the Romantics did not care for Johnson very much.

5 Politics and society

Neither the political nor the social world was the prime object of Johnson's attention. By nature deeply religious, he was a moralist by avocation. He took a keen interest in the world around him, and observed the course of public life through the reigns of the first three Georges. He was also numerate and alive to the developments of science. But his human concerns centred on the individual rather than society in the mass. This bent of mind is seen especially in his obsessive preoccupation with the activities of the human mind—broadly speaking what we should today call psychology. This is in turn connected with an exceptional knowledge, for a layman, of the medical lore of his time, a fact which gains added relevance because of Johnson's own medical and psychological history.

Politics

Johnson made only a small contribution to the formal literature of politics. This took the form principally of four pamphlets which he wrote in support of ministerial positions during the 1770s. In addition he compiled semi-fictional versions of the proceedings in parliament in the early 1740s, and was probably responsible for much of the topical comment in the *Literary Magazine* in the later 1750s. Beyond that, his views on politics have to be disinterred from the mass of his writing on other subjects, for example, his early biographies of prominent figures, his remarks on public literature such as that of Milton, occasional *Rambler* papers, his letters, and the evidence of biographers. It has been argued that these combine to demonstrate an intense awareness of the significance of political issues; but it remains the case that he wrote no full-scale work of political theory. We can more easily locate his precise views on the place of law and medicine in the range of human enquiries (matters touched on later in this chapter) than we can find a coherent statement of his political convictions. None the less, the attempt must be made.

It is natural to start from biographical evidence, though it does not yield conclusive facts. Johnson grew up in Lichfield, a cathedral town with some standing as a provincial centre. It might be expected that we should find a Tory complexion to such a town, especially as it was not a city with very extensive trade. However, there was always a strong Whig element among the town's most prominent citizens, including the ecclesiastical bureaucracy connected with the diocese. For Johnson, a key figure here was Gilbert Walmesley, an official of the church court, who was one of his first intellectual mentors. Much later Johnson wrote of Walmesley: 'He was a whig, with all the virulence and malevolence of his party; yet difference of opinion did not keep us apart' (LOP 1. 81). Then Johnson moved on to the strongly High Church university of Oxford; we know virtually nothing of his political sympathies at this date, but his lifelong streak of rebelliousness could easily have set him against the prevailing order. He had been irreligious in his teens, and quite possibly he was apolitical as a young man.

When he came up to London he soon entered the shabby purlieus of the hack writers. In party terms they were mostly vehement opponents of the Walpole ministry, but then so was a considerable section of the intelligentsia and a substantial portion of Whigs in parliament. Johnson's years as a journalist show him gradually sloughing off the automatic anti-Walpole positions he had at first adopted. His reports of the proceedings in parliament, written between 1740 and 1742, under the guise of debates in the senate of Lilliput, hold some interest as they chronicle significant events leading up to the ultimate fall of Robert Walpole. But they are relatively even-handed, and the obliquity of Johnson's Swiftian *mise-en-scène* does not make it a simple matter to disentangle his own view. It is true that *Marmor Norfolciense* (1739), a mock-archeological discovery, and *A Complete Vindication of the Licensers of the Stage* (1739), an ironic endorsement of the theatrical censorship bill, are routine items in the Opposition campaign against Walpole. But his first major work, the satire in imitation of Juvenal entitled *London* (1738), is already deflected into many non-political issues. The familiar shibboleths are present (Walpole's excise scheme, and his reluctance to wage war on Spain in defence of British commercial interests), but many of the best and most Johnsonian touches concern society at large—'a female atheist talks you dead', 'warbling eunuchs fill a licensed stage' (castrati in the Italian opera), and masquerades do as much damage to the nation as excise schemes. Ostensibly a picture of the political culture engendered by Walpole's long rule, with 'special juries' serving to limit individual freedom, the poem is nowhere near as effective as Pope's Horatian imitations (actually a more direct source of inspiration than Juvenal) in creating a believable portrait of a viciously policed and oppressive state. Johnson appears melodramatic beside Pope when he tries to depict the crimes of the rapacious Orgilio, erecting showy mansions on the backs of the poor. But there is a note of much greater conviction when Johnson turns to poverty itself, and describes his friend Thales (a figure with some resemblance to Savage) as obliged 'through the world a wretched vagrant [to] roam,|For where can starving merit find a home?' The truth seems to be that Johnson was most personally engaged when he touched on his own feelings as an outsider, a provincial, a poor man in a city where riches counted, and a kind of freak. *London* has all the rhetorical signs of a straight Opposition diatribe, but its moments of highest eloquence are less concerned with current party squabbles than with the fate of talent in a world of successful mediocrity. As in the *Life of Savage*, we are aware of Johnson as a Rastignac eager to find a way of making it in the hostile city, rather than a committed ideologue brandishing theories of the public weal.

Of Johnson's obscure middle years little can usefully be said, except to remark that his unexplained absences without known leave in 1745 and 1746 do not indicate that he was away with the invading Jacobite army. Again, Johnson did not write very much explicitly about the Stuart cause; the indications are that he was a lukewarm adherent of the first two Hanoverians, and a more enthusiastic supporter of George III. Some scholars have seen a lingering affection for the ideology of Jacobitism, which can at times be distinguished from a wholehearted commitment to the Catholic and Scottish pretenders themselves. It is true that Johnson held a view of English history in which some of the seventeenth-century promoters of the Stuart cause held a high place; it is now known that his extensive revisions of the

Dictionary for the 1773 edition incorporated a sweeping influx of Stuart sympathizers, largely from among seventeenth-century theologians. But this is very far from showing that he supported the armed insurrections in 1715 and 1745, and there is not a shred of evidence that he lifted a hand to aid Charles Edward, let alone trooped off (as John Buchan's fetching tale, *Midwinter*, suggests) to give the Pretender's forces the benefit of his brain and brawn.

During the mid-1750s Johnson took an active share in running the *Literary Magazine*, and his contributions suggest that his political opinions had developed in some interesting ways. Johnson was opposed on most issues to the Duke of Newcastle, and then when Wiliam Pitt the elder came to power in 1757 he expressed considerable reservations concerning the conduct of the Seven Years War. He was temperamentally at odds with Pitt, whose histrionic gestures, populist rhetoric, and personal ambition all alienated one who inherited traditional humanist ideas of statesmanship. In retrospect it can be argued that Johnson misunderstood the nature of the contests being played out; his economic opinions remained almost mercantilist, and he set little store by international trade, the basis of Britain's wealth in generations to come. His attitude to colonial expansion was coloured by his outrage at exploitation of native peoples (mainly, though not entirely, manifest in the Spanish conquests of America), which carried over into a rooted aversion to the British colonists in North America. He wanted to see Britain's historic enemy France held in check, which was a prime object of the entire war, but he did not relish all the means, military or diplomatic, which were necessary to this end. Johnson's position in these matters is perfectly consistent. He genuinely did sympathize with the oppressed peoples in the colonies, and his deliberately provocative toast to the next insurrection of the slaves in the West Indies reflects an authentic current of feeling. Boswell, who had espoused the cause of the 'brave Corsicans', found this attitude hard to stomach, and predictably took the other side from his revered friend on the question of American independence— Johnson had no time for the colonists' claim for separate status. At the same time Johnson exhibited his usual generosity when he pleaded for humane treatment towards French prisoners of war ('It is far from certain, that a single Englishman will suffer by the charity to the French'—W 12. 79).

The award of a royal pension to Johnson in 1762 complicated his position, and also our interpretation of his stance. It has been suggested that Johnson may have been incapacitated by his beliefs for any 'place of trust', meaning that political office was debarred because Johnson could not conscientiously have taken the oath of allegiance to the crown. This seems unlikely. He did not otherwise identify himself as a nonjuror, and there is a good deal of circumstantial evidence that by this time he was a loyal subject of George III. Whatever general affection he may possibly have felt for the Stuart cause, he had no illusions about the limitations of individual Stuart monarchs. In any case, the pension did not require him to do anything (it was a reward for past services), and did not involve taking any oaths. We are told by someone in a position to know that 'Johnson had conceived a strong prejudice against Lord Bute' (William Shaw, A 40); Bute was at this juncture the much-hated prime minister. Accepting the pension does not seem to have involved any direct commitment to any shade of political opinion. It is also worth noting a letter written by Johnson's printer friend, William Strahan, who was an MP, to a Treasury official; this dates from 1771. Strahan recommends that Johnson should be supported for a seat in parliament by the ministry, now led by Lord North, and observes that he would be 'ready to vindicate such measures as tended to promote the stability of government . . . To the friends of the King you will find him a lamb, to his enemies a lion' (B 2. 138). There is not a hint that Johnson will be in difficulties regarding the qualifying oaths.

It was in the 1770s that Johnson emerged as a political pamphleteer. He wrote four short pieces in support of the ministry, first that headed by the Duke of Grafton (the target of Junius) and then that of Lord North. All of them represent broadly conservative positions. The first, *The False Alarm* (1770), defends the government and parliamentary majority for their conduct in ejecting John Wilkes from the House of Commons. Closely and subtly argued, it shows Johnson in the comfortable role of constitutional lawyer, and is perhaps the most effective of the four items in its trenchant analysis of the controversy which had attended Wilkes's expulsion. A much shorter piece, *The Patriot* (1774), argues that no man was a patriot 'who justified the ridiculous claims of American usurpation [and] endeavours to deprive the nation of its natural and lawful authority over its own colonies' (Y 10. 396). It was succeeded by *Taxation no Tyranny* (1775), pouring scorn on the claims of the colonial population of North America to be exempt from British taxation. In the meantime, Johnson had also written *Thoughts on the Late Transactions Respecting Falkland's Islands* (1771), which supported the ministerial line on this perennially thorny problem—that is, whether to accept 'actual possession' of the islands by agreement with Spain, without settling the longer-term 'question of right' (Y 10. 367).

It will be no surprise to reach a conclusion that Johnson's politics were complex and evolved over time. He can certainly not be regarded as a twentieth-century Tory, as Donald Greene has pointed out in the most searching and thorough discussion of the subject. On the other hand, it would be wrong to dismiss as mere persiflage comments such as: 'Now you know every bad man is a Whig; every man who has loose notions' (B 5. 271). If he was less than fully serious in defining 'Whig' in his *Dictionary* as 'the name of a faction', there is abundant evidence that on the big questions of Church and State which divided the nation he belonged to the opposite sect. Even though the Tories were long under proscription and a nugatory force in Parliament, there did remain a core of Tory ideology in sections of the population at large. In the heyday of Sir Lewis Namier it used to be accepted that ideology was not a large part of the driving mechanism of English politics in the mid-eighteenth century. But a new generation of historians have shown that 'Britain remained at grass roots a xenophobic nation, resentful of foreign kings, whig corruption, papists and dissenters, and doggedly, if largely passively, loyal to the Stuarts, the supremacy of the Church of England and to traditional views of divine right' (Nicholas Phillipson). Johnson had abjured divine right, and there is, as remarked, no evidence that he even flirted with Jacobitism. But he assuredly believed in the supremacy of the Church of England; he had his share of xenophobia; and he hated Whig corruption, dissenters, and papists as cordially as the next man. (It is worth adding that many popular riots from the time of Sacheverell were led by self-identified Tories.)

Unless we cling to an unreconstructed Namierite position, it can hardly be doubted that a strong body of Tory sentiment survived for many decades after the Tories ceased to be a considerable force in Westminster politics. This was a Toryism not confined to the scattering of country gentlemen who led a marginal life in parliament as knights of the shire; it extended to artisans and tradesmen, to clerics and intellectuals, even to some in the City of London. Johnson would never have been a dependable adherent of a Tory party, if modern parties had existed to permit such a thing. His natural independence and his taste for kicking over the traces would have precluded tame support of a single-minded political agenda. But of course it was partly his streak of rebelliousness, his refusal to conform, and his scorn for the powerful which led him into opposition to the Whig magnates who ruled the land. Many components went into his political make-up: intense piety and affection for the Church, sympathy for the underdog, reverence for the past, loyalty to the institution of monarchy, a hatred of cruelty, a belief in the native virtues of the British nation, a fear of the unknown, and a fondness for what was closest to home. This combination of attributes does not add up to an obvious label in terms of later political groupings, but in the eighteenth century it easily translated itself into what contemporaries recognized as a Tory. In that carefully defined sense, it is an adequate working description of Samuel Johnson.

In connection with Johnson's friend Edmund Burke, J. H. Plumb has written: 'Although a gifted and ambitious man could move about eighteenth-century English society with ease, he could never feel that deep sense of belonging that came naturally to those born within it.' This circumstance explains a great deal about Johnson as well, and especially his political identity. A lonely and tormented man, he longed to associate himself with larger aggregations of people, and to lose himself in the normality of everyday living. It does not require any advanced psychological theory to see why this might produce violent oscillations between extreme orthodoxy and intense radicalism—why the same man might be a humanitarian on prison conditions and a hard-liner on penal reform. There are times when Johnson's views and phrasing come close to those of the outrageous political writer John Shebbeare, who had stood in the pillory for his controversial

Tory works. Boswell tells us that 'Johnson and Shebbeare were frequently named together', as no firm adherents of the early Hanoverian monarchs, and as fellow recipients of a pension from George III (B 4. 113). It has always been regarded as an absurd conjunction, but we are misled by our cosily respectable image of the great Dr Johnson. To many contemporaries he was a gadfly, a nuisance, a fellow of no breeding—Horace Walpole refused even to be introduced to him. That was what you risked, once you stepped outside the stockade of Whig conformism.

Johnson's supposed high-Tory beliefs are not a canard put about by Boswell, Mrs Piozzi, or for that matter Macaulay. Many contemporaries who read his works and listened regularly to what he had to say came to the same conclusion over his political standpoint. To take one example, Thomas Tyers asserted without apparent fear of contradiction that 'Johnson's high tory principles in church and state were well known' (JM 2. 346). It would certainly be unwise to lay too much stress on his conversational asides. Palpably, a measure of comic hyperbole enters into such statements as: 'I have always said, the first Whig was the Devil' (B 3. 326). But the people who surrounded Johnson and noted down his sayings knew that as well as we do. Unless we are peculiarly self-deceived, we must recognize that Boswell understood the tone and drift of Johnson's humour as well as anyone who ever lived. The idea that Johnson might constantly make comments of pointed irony which Boswell took *au pied de la lettre* is itself a ravishingly comic notion.

Society

A man with the broad humanity of Johnson necessarily responded to many of the social issues of his day. Nevertheless, he wrote comparatively little which had as its frontal concern the state of contemporary society. Only one work within this category can be regarded as among his finest productions, and that was formally a review of a work on metaphysics, Soame Jenyns's *Free Enquiry into the Nature and Origin of Evil* (1757). For the rest, we have scattered observations on a variety of topics, ranging from crime and philanthropy to education and the position of women. His incidental comments always carry a good deal of interest, as, for example, what he says about education in one of the best of the many prefaces he wrote for the work of others, that is, the introduction to an autodidact's manual called *The Preceptor* (1748). He also contributed a thoughtful preface to a dictionary of trade and commerce in 1761, a subject on which he was well grounded.

However, we all know that he was a considerable human-itarian, and the primary evidence for this is biographical. The most obvious example of his practical concern for the dis-advantaged can be found in his own household. This strange collection of misfits and waifs was gradually assimilated into the Johnsonian ménage. Hester Thrale's private note on this assembly is assuredly unkind in tone, but appears to be not far from the truth:

He [Robert Levet] lived with Johnson as a sort of *necessary man*, or surgeon to the wretched household he had in Bolt Court, where blind Mrs Williams, dropsical Mrs Desmoulins, black Francis and his white wife's bastard with a wretched Mrs White, and a thing that he called Poll, shared his bounty and increased his dirt. Levet used to bleed one, and blister another, and be very useful, though I believe very disagreeable to all. (T 1. 531–2)

Thoroughly disagreeable itself, this record at least possesses the merit of showing what most people from respectable society thought about the matter. We need to be reminded of this in order to gauge Johnson's sheer courage in maintaining such a domestic arena. There is no stronger proof of his utter disdain for the polite and heartless code of his betters. Fanny Burney wrote with flinching amazement of a house 'filled and overrun with all sorts of strange creatures, who he admits from mere charity, and because nobody else will admit them—for his charity is unbounded—or rather, bounded only by his circumstances' (D&L 1. 114).

It should be enough to fill out this cast-list with brief biographies. Anna Williams was a poet of moderate talent; Johnson arranged for her miscellaneous works to be published in 1766, eked out by contributions from himself and Mrs Thrale, who later described it as 'a thin flat quarto which...sold miserably'. Mrs Williams was the daughter of a deranged projector whose career reads like the synopsis of a *Rambler* character-sketch of misapplied learning. She had cataracts in both eyes before she was 30 and was totally blind by the time she was 35. Elizabeth Desmoulins was the daughter of Johnson's godfather Samuel Swinfen; she had been a friend of Tetty, but after her fellow-lodger married Johnson she fell on hard times and was reduced to menial occupations. Francis Barber was a slave boy from Jamaica, apparently known by the name of Quashey in plantation records, who was brought to England to live in the family of Dr Richard Bathurst, a close friend of Johnson. He was about 10 when he entered Johnson's service after the death of Tetty, and apart from a short break when he ran away to sea (some say he was press-ganged) he remained with his master until the old man died in 1784. Poll Carmichael was very likely a former prostitute. Johnson once called her 'a stupid slut' and, in a memorable if slightly obscure phrase, 'wigglewaggle' (D&L 1. 116). Yet he exerted himself on her behalf, as he did on those of others. Levet was a medical practitioner to the poor, excluded from the ranks of the medical establishment but capable of bringing aid and comfort to the sick, as Johnson's great elegy on him reveals.

Only the most disingenuous observer would pretend that these were an easy group to get along with, individually or collectively. Even Johnson himself could not conceal his impatience with their antics in a letter to Mrs Thrale: 'Williams hates everybody; Levet hates Desmoulins, and does not love Williams; Desmoulins hates them both; Poll loves none of them.' (L 2. 268) Frank Barber is exempt from criticism here; he is the most attractive in the whole *galère*, but then he was rising in the world, and the others were clearly going down: Johnson expressed his faith in Frank by making him his residuary legatee. Johnson helped to support others, including the mentally retarded daughter of a cousin. The numerous acts of kindness he performed towards these people testify both to his liberality of spirit and his unconcern for the opinion of the world. They were, above all, poor; and he had never forgotten what that was like.

It is very far from trivial to recall that he displayed kindness of this sort in all sorts of situations. He would thrust pennies into the hands of poor children asleep in doorways and streets (JM 2.

251). His humane attitude towards women of the town emerges from the pages of Boswell, who had to equivocate a good deal in view of his own regular recourse to prostitutes. Even the kindness Johnson showed towards his cat may seem more significant when we encounter an *Idler* paper (no. 17) attacking animal experimentation as 'horrid operations'. He supported charities actively, but was not afraid to attack the governors of the Foundling Hospital for neglecting religious instruction of their charges, forgetting as they did that irreligion might be 'equally pernicious with gin and tea'; they ought, Johnson urges, to 'consider a little the minds, as well as the bodies, of the children' (W 11. 252). Official displeasure was voiced, and there was talk of a prosecution for criminal libel. As usual, Johnson stuck to his guns, and wrote another pamphlet, repeating that none of the children he had met 'appeared to have heard of the catechism' (W 11. 261). We find the same combination of rigour and compassion in his *Rambler* papers on prostitution and in his real-life dealings with disadvantaged people. In his support of the convicted forger Dr Dodd, Johnson urged clemency without palliating the crime.

It would be glib to suggest that this capacity to sympathize with outcasts derives from Johnson's own sense of himself as someone who did not fully belong within respectable society. However, we can safely say that any life of hardship elicited his ready identification. Thus, he was moved to say a good deal on behalf of soldiers and seamen, as evidenced by a piece like his essay 'On the Bravery of the English Common Soldiers' (1760), exploring a 'plebian magnanimity' scarcely to be expected of the common people ('We can show a peasantry of heroes', W 12. 81). It would be consoling to think that this sympathy for the underprivileged extended to an advanced conception of the need to open up opportunities for women, who still endured a variety of civil disabilities and social restrictions. Indeed, according to Frances Reynolds, he 'set a higher value upon female friendship than ... most men' (JM 2. 252). But though Johnson liked and admired many individual women, respected the achievements of Charlotte Lennox, Elizabeth Carter, and others, and depended more deeply on Hester Thrale than on any other human being in the latter half of his life, he was never able to transcend the assumptions of his age. Nekayah is given an unusually free-running role in *Rasselas*, and a few papers in the *Rambler* are devoted to a cumbrous attempt to present the woman's point of view, but there are many occasions when Johnson falls back on the routine dogmas of patriarchalism. There is a strict limit to his 'liberalism' in most social questions. Neither, for that matter, did he enter very closely into the savage mind. He attempted to peep beyond the barricades of civilized life when he investigated the 'primitive' life of the Highlands, and succeeded extraordinarily well for the most part; but the ordinary racial beliefs of his time came into play when he considered the culture of remote South Sea islanders or American Indians.

By common consent the greatest of his shorter works in prose is the review he wrote in 1757 of a book by Soame Jenyns, his *Free Enquiry* attempting a fresh answer to the problem of evil. It is Jenyns's lasting misfortune to have incurred such a withering reply, since he was a mostly inoffensive and decent, if untalented, writer. Johnson produced the most blistering attack on Augustan complacencies which the century witnessed—not even Voltaire wrote anything more conclusive or more remorseless. The strongest scorn is reserved for what Jenyns says in his bumbling, well-meaning way about poverty, arguing that the deprivations of this state are alleviated by the absence of fears and cares, along with 'a more exquisite relish of the smallest enjoyments'. Johnson disposes of this argument with a series of devastating retorts:

Poverty is very gently paraphrased by *want of riches* ... This author and Pope perhaps never saw the miseries which they imagine thus easy to be borne ... The compensations of sickness I have never found near to equivalence, and the transports of recovery only prove the intenseness of the pain ... Though it should be granted that those who are *born to poverty and drudgery* should not be *deprived* by an *improper education* of the *opiate* of *ignorance*; even this concession will not be of much use to direct our practice, unless it be determined who are those that are *born to poverty*. (W 12. 286–8)

Johnson must have felt himself at least born to drudgery, if not absolutely to poverty, but his concerns here go well beyond crude self-identification. 'I am always afraid of determining on the side of envy or cruelty', he concludes (W 12. 289). The rage is not simulated; it proceeds from a well-established sense of the peculiarly bad taste left in the mouth by arguments like that of Jenyns, which disregard real deprivation as they invent imaginary consolations. As Hannah More reported: 'He hated to hear people whine about metaphysical distresses, when there was so much want and hunger in the world' (JM 1. 477). The most famous passage in the review occurs a short while later, when Johnson responds to a fanciful conceit by Jenyns, to the effect that there may be some higher beings who treat humans as we treat the lower animal kingdom. The idea kindles Johnson's most impassioned writing—'To swell a man with a tympany [dropsy] is as good sport as to blow a frog' (W 12. 299). Once more we see that the highest powers are called out in this writer when pain and distress are in question. About suffering, Johnson was seldom wrong.

One specialized branch of social inquiry needs to be mentioned in conclusion. Johnson somehow attained a considerable knowledge of the law, and a great jurist actually suggested that he might well have been Lord Chancellor if the opportunities had arisen (B 3. 310). Boswell regularly consulted him on legal issues, even though he was a qualified barrister and Johnson a layman, and despite the fact that the cases often involved the Scottish courts, with their very different rules. The most extensive result of this interest came in the assistance which Johnson lent to his young friend Robert Chambers in preparing the Vinerian Lectures to be delivered at Oxford; from around 1766 to 1770 Johnson devoted much of his time to work on these lectures, which Chambers had to give as the successor of William Blackstone as Vinerian Professor of Common Law.

The text of these lectures has now been edited by Thomas Curley (1986), but it remains impossible to be sure exactly what share was ghost-written by Johnson: the collaboration was naturally a closely guarded secret, totally unknown to Boswell as it was to most of Johnson's closest friends. However, even if it would be rash to extrapolate too directly from the lectures to ascertain Johnson's exact opinions on points of common law, at least our knowledge of this work enables us to get some sense of the place of legal discourse in what Johnson assembled as the conversation of mankind. Furthermore, we can see that the forensic skill of his criticism, and the logical thrust of his arguments (whether in writing or in speech), derive from more than an amateur's dabbling in stray episodes from the courts. Johnson had thought out the principles of the subject, as he had of almost everything else.

Medicine and psychology

Johnson, reported Hester Thrale, 'had studied medicine diligently in all its branches, but had given particular attention to the diseases of the imagination, which he watched in himself with a solicitude destructive of his own peace' (A 86). On another occasion she drew attention to the ministrations he performed on behalf of others as a kind of lay physician, suggesting he was 'tempted no little to the sin of quackery' (T 1. 197). It has often been noticed that Johnson displayed a concern with mental health (his own and that of others) which can scarcely be paralleled in any major writer before the time of Freud. Earlier than most, he realized the intimate connection between mind and body in most forms of sickness, observing that 'there is no distemper not in the highest degree acute, upon which the mind has not some influence' (L 1. 280). It is therefore appropriate to look briefly at Johnson's medical background and the bearing this has on his work.

His contacts with the medical profession were surprisingly extensive. He was named after his godfather, Samuel Swinfen, a physician who lodged in the Johnson household; much later, he took Swinfen's daughter into his own complicated group of live-in dependants. The wider family circle of his boyhood also included the notable physician Sir John Floyer. A schoolfellow, Edmund Hector, was to become a Birmingham surgeon and a lifelong friend. Another schoolmate was Robert James, who was to produce a major *Medicinal Dictionary* for which Johnson wrote proposals and possibly a few entries. Later medical advisers included Thomas Lawrence and William Heberden, who were among the most prominent physicians of the day. He also had some dealings with successful practitioners like Sir Lucas Pepys and Sir Richard Jebb. He knew some figures lower down in the scale of medical respectability; his own father had sold patent remedies, as did most booksellers, and he worked for John Newbery, a publisher who did much to expand the range of children's literature while maintaining a profitable sideline in James's celebrated fever powders.

Robert Levet was the most important of Johnson's contacts in this world, one of the breed of humble practitioners, combining basic medical care with simple surgery and the work of an apothecary or pharmacist, who picked up his knowledge in almost the same hand-to-mouth way as Oliver Goldsmith, and never gained serious accreditation in the jealously guarded world of the medical profession, whose upper echelons were occupied by graduates of Oxford and Cambridge. But Johnson was well aware that there was more to the art of healing than letters after one's name, as his lines in tribute to Levet indicate, by means of a daring pun:

> Yet still he fills affection's eye.
> Obscurely wise, and coarsely kind;
> Nor lettered arrogance deny
> Thy praise to merit unrefined.

Levet was a surly, awkward man with few social skills, but he was a member of Johnson's household for twenty years up to his death, and he must have done much good among his poor patients in that period. Like other irregulars, and even some of the outright quacks, he concentrated on results rather than following the passing therapeutic theories which directed the fashionable end of the market. Johnson's superbly simple and eloquent verses celebrate not just an individual life but a whole commitment to duty within a 'narrow round', enlisting the parable of the 'single talent well employed'. Levet is described as 'Of every friendless name the friend'; his was 'the power of art without the show'. In his unsnobbish way Johnson manages to ennoble Levet's humble avocation without patronizing the simple people who were his patients. Levet's career becomes the paradigm of a good life led within confined circumstances and guided by a single-minded attention to duty and virtue.

There is, however, another reason, apart from his range of friends, which accounts for Johnson's special interest in medical matters. It happens that he himself endured a complex history of physical and mental disorders. He suffered from scrofula, probably blindness in one eye, defective hearing in old age, and what was diagnosed as asthma. In his last years he endured emphysema, a sarcocele, and dropsy. He had a stroke in 1783, leading to temporary aphasia. Throughout his life he displayed strange tics and contortions which have been variously diagnosed by modern authorities. As for his psychological problems, they ranged from protracted sleeplessness to intense feelings of guilt and worthlessness. He underwent at least two full-scale breakdowns, as a young man and in middle life. His psychological problems may have extended into the sexual area. References in his correspondence to Mrs Thrale, and the survival among her property of 'Dr Johnson's padlock', have prompted suggestions that he asked her to indulge him in masochistic practices. Most recent commentators have dismissed this theory as untenable. We might be glad to feel that there was nothing in the story, but the truth is that firm evidence has not been adduced to dispose of it with assurance. It does not, perhaps, matter very much. We know with absolute certainty that Johnson suffered deeply and that he had a massive deficiency in self-esteem, owning to some ingrained or acquired blows to his psyche. Boswell thought his 'vile melancholy' (B 1. 35) was hereditary; others have put it down to problems in relating to his parents (or to guilt about those problems). Whatever the cause, he struggled manfully with pressures which might have disabled others. If, conceivably, yet one more element in his troubled self was a sexual compulsion, that would not make him less admirable or noteworthy.

Johnson wrote a certain amount directly on the subject of medicine. He compiled lives of the great teacher Herman Boerhaave, who established Leiden as the most important medical school in Europe, and produced in 'Boerhaave's men' an influential group of physicians, and of Thomas Sydenham, the English doctor who had developed the scientific study of medical phenomena. (Sydenham had written a treatise on gout, another affliction to which Johnson was subject, at any rate by contemporary definitions of the ailment.) More widely, Johnson's work is pervaded by his interest in what Bacon had called 'the diseases and infirmities of the mind'. In particular, the *Rambler* consistently deals with moral and mental life in terms of imagery drawn from medical language. There was, of course, as yet no terminology of psychiatric lore. As pointed out below (p. 64), Johnson deploys a vocabulary in which words formerly technical or scientific were acquiring transferred senses connected with emotion or psychology. Thus, when he speaks in *Rambler* no. 2 of philosophy boasting of 'her physic of mind, her cathartics of vice, or lenitives of passion', he is trading on this growing tendency of key words to move out of a strict physical sense into an applied and metaphoric area. The 'physic of the mind' exercised in the *Rambler* takes the form of diagnosing common causes of unhappiness and prescribing remedies. Johnson, a bitterly unhappy man for much of his life, respected and valued happiness as the naturally sanguine (itself, by the way, one of the words which were then on the turn) can seldom manage to do.

A lucid and penetrating account of Johnson's medico-psychological regime in his writing has been given by John Wiltshire. A key issue dealt with by Wiltshire is the case-history in madness which is provided in chapters 40 to 47 of *Rasselas*, describing the crazed delusions of power in a solitary astronomer, and the way in which these are dispelled when he re-enters ordinary society, engaging in straightforward converse with the rest of the human race (see above, pp. 43–4). The best-known passage in this episode occurs when Imlac declares: 'No disease of the imagination . . . is so difficult of cure as that which is complicated with a dread of guilt' (Y 16. 162). As often, we can easily discern a trace of self-reference on the author's part. But it is worth remembering that a cure *is* effected in this case. The 'history of a man learning' ends not in the bleak failures charted in *The Vanity of Human Wishes*, but in qualified optimism. The astronomer fears a relapse, but after giving him traditional counsel (to occupy himself with 'business' or harmless dissipations), Imlac concludes: 'Your learning and virtue . . . may justly give you hopes.' In the arena of medicine and psychology, as elsewhere, Johnson offers the prospect of gradual benefit accruing to those who persist and struggle.

6 Language and literature

Johnson was not a great creative writer in the same manner as Shakespeare, Dickens, or Joyce. These are figures of transcendent imaginative power, who mediate an intense personal vision through sharply idiosyncratic dealings with language. They bend, batter, and sculpt words to their purposes. Equally, they operate with a sublime innocence of the limitations which are supposed to define 'normal' usage. Johnson stands at the opposite extreme. His hold on English possesses a deeply impersonal quality: it has to do with obeying, and not transgressing, the normative forms we customarily obey. His approach to words could hardly be less innocent. It is knowledgeable, even knowing, and it starts not from poetic perception (though it may end up there) but from such attributes as common sense, observation, sensitivity to the habitual phrases and rhythms of English—in short, from an acceptance of the everyday communicative needs which language serves. For the great creative feat to be brought off—*King Lear*, *Bleak House*, *Ulysses*, *The Waste Land*—it is often necessary to take words where they have never been before. What Johnson is especially good at is tracing where words *have* been, and in what company; and where they might be likely to go in future.

Johnson's linguistic views are scattered over a wide range of his works. But a group of sources exists, which reveals most clearly his ideas on the subject. First there is the *Dictionary* of 1755, together with the Plan which had been published eight years earlier, as a trial kite flown to test the interest of public and patrons. Quite apart from the entries themselves, we can invoke the eloquent Preface to the *Dictionary*. Secondly, Johnson's periodical essays, notably the *Rambler*, devote some space to linguistic matters. Thirdly, Johnson's works of formal literary criticism, above all the *Lives of the Poets*, show him at work on English used at the highest level, under the pressure of demanding creative exigencies, in works by Milton, Dryden, Swift, and Pope. Even more important is Johnson's lifelong concern with

Shakespeare, culminating (but not actually concluding) in his edition of the dramatist in 1765. Lastly, there is external evidence supplied by the observations of contemporaries, descriptions of Johnson's written and spoken style, satires, parodies, and the like. This last category obviously has to be handled with care, because not all the witnesses are disinterested or reliable. But they do record an important part of the Johnson legacy, in that they show how people thought the Great Cham had influenced the course of the English language. Their observations are often interesting, even when they seem to us misguided.

Johnson's own written style deserves attention. His principal area of interest, according to his biographer Arthur Murphy, was 'general philology' (JM 1. 363). This means a little more than linguistics in the technical sense, but it does point to the study of good letters which lay at the heart of education in earlier centuries. The characteristic style was thrust into prominence by the *Dictionary*, where some critics found an unduly hospitable attitude to barbarous polysyllabic coinages, especially words of a technical philosophic or scientific cast. The *Rambler* had already displayed this learned and weighty diction in active use. Nor was the employment of ponderous Latinate words its only distinguishing mark, for there are favourite devices of syntax and rhythm (parallelism, antithesis, inversion, and so on) which are just as important in obtaining the effects Johnson is seeking. None the less, most of the critics fixed on the supposedly abstract, general, 'Latin', and pompous character of his language. For Charles Churchill, Johnson became Pomposo: 'Who, to increase his native strength | Draws words, six syllables in length.' He was mocked as the English Lexiphanes, who promoted 'the Babylonish dialect which learned pedants much affect', in a savage parody of his 'hard words and affected style'. More amusingly, Horace Walpole wrote to a friend of Johnson's 'teeth-breaking diction', and a few years later claimed: 'He prefers learned words to the simple and common—and on every occasion. He is never simple, elegant, or light.' Macaulay said much the same thing in 1831: 'All his books are written in a learned language, in a language which nobody hears from his mother or his nurse, a language in which nobody ever quarrels, or drives bargains, or makes love, a language in which nobody ever thinks.'

To these objections there are many possible lines of reply. Johnson himself proffered some of these retorts, as when he told Boswell on Skye, 'I am not answerable for all the words in my Dictionary' (B 5. 273). Boswell had shown him verses in a magazine 'composed of uncommon words' taken from the *Dictionary*. To recognize the truth of Johnson's riposte is to see the injustice of another contemporary claim, that he had written his own works in order to make the *Dictionary* necessary. The job of the lexicographer was to create a public instrument for general use, and though Johnson was an unashamedly prescriptive lexicographer, grading words by their register and associations, he did not invent the stock of words which were to be described.

In the twentieth century a widespread admiration for Johnson has brought with it a re-examination of his style. The scholar W. K. Wimsatt produced two important books, *The Prose Style of Samuel Johnson* (1941) and *Philosophic Words* (1948), which helped to dispel Macaulay's crude estimate. We now recognize that Johnson can employ generalized constructions with a quasi-concrete force and particularity; this applies both to his poetry and his prose. We see, too, that his 'philosophic' diction is an excitingly poetic use of scientific words just losing their strict literal sense and becoming metaphoric. In this context we should note an important passage in the Preface to the *Dictionary*, beginning: 'As by the cultivation of various sciences, a language is amplified, it will be more furnished with words deflected from their original sense . . .' (W 10. 62). Words found in the *Dictionary* (many of them used in the *Rambler*) include such items as 'attraction', 'diffusion', 'elasticity', 'relaxation', 'corrosion', 'ingredient', 'volatility', 'acrimony', 'exacerbation', 'irritation', 'mortification', 'plethora', 'ebullition', and 'composition'. All of these in the time of Bacon, who is frequently used to provide illustrative examples, were literal, physical, medical, chemical, or biological terms. Nowadays most of them occur more commonly in transferred senses, as in the psychological usage of a word like 'relaxation'. Johnson caught them just, as it were, on the slide. It is because they still carry their older scientific overtones—now lost to us in a word like 'relaxation'—that they possess a unique point and resonance in Johnson's hands.

It is this enlistment of the decayed half-life of words which gives energy to much of Johnson's writing. Take, for example, a passage from his pamphlet on the Falkland Islands affair:

The caprices of voluntary agents laugh at calculation. It is not always that there is a strong reason for a great event. Obstinacy and flexibility, malignity and kindness, give place alternately to each other, and the reason of these vicissitudes, however important may be the consequences, often escapes the mind in which the change is made. (Y 10. 366)

We see here, as in the prose of a writer who learnt much from Johnson, Jane Austen, that what initially look like empty abstractions turn out to be forceful expressions with a real semantic kick of their own. More generally, we can say that the hidden life in Johnson's style comes from his awareness of the potential of dead metaphor and of the buried imagery in commonplace phrases. Thus, he is able to make conversational sport with a threadbare old expression, 'a dog in a doublet' (B 3. 329).

We need not, then, be surprised that Boswell praised his mentor for his 'splendour of images' and for his 'brilliancy of fancy' (B 2. 335; 4. 116). He meant a quality of enlivening discourse by raising the ghosts of historic meaning in abstract-looking words. As Donald Greene has stressed, Johnson valued the faculty in poets of creating 'pictures to the mind' (LOP 1. 51), and his best writing exhibits the same sense of language as a dynamic force as does his appraisal of the subject in the Preface to the *Dictionary*, where he observes that 'words ... when they are not gaining strength ... are generally losing it' (W 10. 62). He knew that change was always on the point of undoing the seeming fixity of the English language, and he came to realize that it was vain to attempt to arrest this process. By the same token, his own style reflects an awareness that words carry with them a little of their history, as a sort of unexploded charge which the writer (if he or she is up to it) can set off in a controlled detonation. The more we read his works, the more we learn to uncover the swift imaginative leaps, the slyly concealed jokes, and the solid connecting fibres that lie beneath the surface of apparently ordinary words.

The Dictionary

Johnson's *Dictionary of the English Language* was soon recognized as 'a kind of national work' which justified the award of a royal pension. David Hume, who did not often see eye to eye with Johnson, said as much to Boswell in 1762. It attained unprecedented authority, and remained the bedrock of English lexicography until the *Oxford English Dictionary* began to appear more than a century later. It was the first work which had fully harnessed Johnson's gifts—his learning, his capacity to marshal detail in a large overall design, his sensitivity to the history and associations of words and phrases, his literary taste. He had written two significant items already, the poem *London* and the biography of Savage, when he embarked on the most sustained work of his life. It brought him fame and recognition. There is also a sense in which Johnson unlocked a powerful part of his literary personality as he worked on the task; some of the benefit can be seen in the linguistic energy of the *Rambler* and the *Adventurer* in the early 1750s, where it almost seems that Johnson has discovered for the first time the full stylistic armoury at his command.

The surprising thing is that its author needed less than ten years to compile the *Dictionary*. Offhandedly he told Boswell that 'he had taken longer time than he needed to have done in composing his Dictionary' (B 1. 443): in the original journal entry Boswell has the additional phrase 'through idleness', an explanation which was taken out of Johnson's remarks in the published *Life*. Most people would have been proud to accomplish so much virtually single-handed, even without considering the quality of the work performed. The six amanuenses fulfilled the tasks of a modern photocopying machine and little more. Simply to manage this team of assistants—mostly frustrated writers—called for some skill and patience.

A contract was signed with the booksellers in June 1746 and work on the *Dictionary* proper began within a few months from this date, as at least one of the copyists was already on the payroll. Johnson had a special interleaved copy of an existing dictionary made up, into which his own entries could be incorporated. His method of assembling the illustrative quotations was to skim rapidly through books, marking the words and contexts so that the amanuenses could transcribe them on to small slips of paper, which were filed ready for Johnson to pick his way through them and select the right examples for his purpose. The opening sheets, covering A to the beginning of C, were printed off by 1750, but it emerged that the coverage was too bulky in these portions and a less discursive manner had to be adopted. An important recent study by Allen Reddick has suggested that this amounted to a completely false start, and that a major crisis in composition needed to be overcome around 1750 before Johnson could resume his work, utilizing different means of organization and selection of his materials. In the event, all the sheets for the first volume were printed off by early 1754. Johnson was now well advanced in putting together the second volume; he had left until last the preface, the history of the language, and the grammar, which were not written until the summer of 1754. Printing of the second volume, covering letters L to Z, was now under way. The final hurdle was a successful application to Oxford for an MA degree, to be blazoned on the title-page: thus, Johnson finally gained access to the academic honours which were his due, and which had been denied to him by his enforced departure from the university a quarter of a century before. The man who had dropped out in the shadow of poverty was now to produce an intellectual tool of unequalled importance for eighteenth-century English culture. The most closely comparable achievement from an Oxford scholar is the legal *Commentaries* of William Blackstone, another codifying and synthesizing masterpiece which Johnson must have known well.

The progress of composition can be traced in some detail. It was the publisher Robert Dodsley who contacted Johnson on behalf of the group of sponsoring booksellers, though the idea fell on fertile ground—it had been in his head for some time. In 1746 Johnson wrote a draft 'Scheme' outlining his intended manner of going about the task: this survives in manuscript. Subsequently a revised version was prepared and published in 1747 as *The Plan of a Dictionary of the English Language*: this too had been circulated in manuscript and amended in response to suggestions made, some of them by the *Plan*'s dedicatee, Lord Chesterfield. Johnson received £10 from the earl, a generous enough reward for the dedication of such a relatively short book. Unfortunately Chesterfield then apparently lost interest, and when Johnson went calling on him was found to be not available. Eventually, when the *Dictionary* was ready for publication, Chesterfield started to take notice again, and puffed the forthcoming volumes in a periodical. But it was too late. Johnson, incensed, produced a stinging rebuke in the form of a lofty repudiation of aristocratic patronage. His letter to Chesterfield, dated 7 February 1755, was widely known in his own lifetime and became still more famous after Boswell obtained a reliable copy, originating from Johnson himself, to use in the *Life* (B 1. 261–3). Since then it has been viewed as a classic statement of authorial independence, marking the juncture when writers finally cast themselves off from servitude. That is too simple a version of literary history, but the letter deserves its renown for its proud but simple eloquence:

Seven years, my Lord, have now passed since I waited in your outward rooms or was repulsed from your door, during which time I have been pushing on my work through difficulties of which it is useless to complain, and have brought it at last to the verge of publication without one act of assistance, one word of encouragement, or one smile of favour. Such treatment I did not expect, for I never had a patron before.

Johnson was paid, over time, £1,575 for his work—a large sum in eighteenth-century terms but hardly excessive in view of the time he had spent. The *Dictionary* was published in two folio volumes on 15 April 1755, a landmark date in the history of the language.

The only substantial revision of the *Dictionary* was that undertaken by Johnson in 1771: he called the task 'a very great work'. This was published as the 'fourth edition' in 1773, still at the original price. Allen Reddick has recently shown that Johnson used the opportunity to augment the doctrinal orthodoxy of his quotations, importing a large number of passages from theologians and pious writers from the High Church end of the ideological spectrum. Some definitions were improved and a fresh look taken at some of the editorial policies governing the entries. The last edition to appear in Johnson's lifetime came out in the closing year of his life; shortly after his death competition began to hot up once more, and further editions in quarto and folio soon followed. Meanwhile the cheaper octavo continued to appear at regular intervals. Around the turn of the century so-called 'supplements' to Johnson started to appear: one by George Mason (1801) accused the original compiler of blunders and inaccuracies in every department. H. J. Todd edited the standard version from

1818; it was doubtless such a recension that Becky Sharp threw out of her coach into Chiswick Mall as a symbol of abandoning the disciplines of childhood.

It is still sometimes asserted that Johnson compiled the first English dictionary. This is very far from the truth; there had been lexicons of a sort for a century and a half, and by the later 1600s there were some capacious and useful efforts in this branch of scholarship. Johnson made use of the better examples, particularly those of the schoolmaster Nathan Bailey, which disputed precedence with Johnson over the next few decades. In terms of general methods, the leading innovation in Johnson consisted of the wealth of illustrative quotations, a practice he had taken from foreign dictionaries such as the *Vocabolario* of the Florentine Academy, as well as the lexicographers of ancient Greek and Latin. Almost equally radical is the system of dividing up entries into an organized series of definitions; something of the sort had been performed by Robert Ainsworth in his Latin *Thesaurus* (1736), one of the important 'hidden' books of the period. It should be noted that Johnson's entries proceed from the radical sense towards the poetic and metaphoric. Unlike the *Oxford English Dictionary*, that is, Johnson does not operate on historical lines; his entries follow a semantic and not a temporal logic.

The coverage of the *Dictionary* can be divided into main text and supporting material. In both areas there is a clear-cut division between successful and unsuccessful operations. In the main series of entries, for example, there is no attempt to render pronunciation (other than stress), which is one of the main things we habitually look for in a dictionary. The etymologies are sometimes more inventive than accurate, and the inclusion or omission of recondite words can be arbitrary at times. On the other hand, the definitions have rarely been improved upon, whilst the quotations supply not just an effective linguistic context but a kind of encyclopaedic survey of the Augustan mind. As regards the supporting material, it is universally agreed that the grammar and history of the language are weak and derivative, though Johnson did his best in matters not fully within his natural intellectual compass—he studied the work of early Saxonists like George Hickes to produce dutiful and competent surveys. The glory of this portion of the work, indeed arguably the outstanding feature of the entire *Dictionary*, is the Preface: eloquent, thoughtful, and still undated in its scrutiny of the implications of linguistic change.

Both the definitions and the quotations carried with them a new authority. 'That damned dictionary-making', said the Corsican patriot Paoli in mock despair. 'He is all definitions.' Certainly Johnson found ways of explaining meanings which turned lexicography from a banal reference function to a kind of imaginative table of equivalences. Significances are weighed out in carefully adjusted quantities: thus 'precarious' is defined:

Dependent; uncertain, because depending on the will of another... No word is more unskilfully used than this with its derivatives. It is used for *uncertain* in all its senses; but it only means uncertain, as dependent on others: thus there are authors who mention the *precariousness* of an *account*, of the *weather*, of a *die*.

Johnson's willingness to grade words for their effect or tone or social register, helps to give his work its highly personal flavour; moreover, it shows his feeling for the company words have kept, and his strong awareness of the role of context in establishing meaning. Everyone knows that the compiler permitted himself some joking definitions, aimed against Whigs, Scotsmen, and patrons, not to mention self-implicating references like the entry for 'lexicographer': 'a writer of dictionaries; a harmless drudge, that busies himself in tracing the original, and detailing the signification of words.' But such relaxations from strict authorial propriety are rare; most of the work is taken up by serious, useful, and apt definitions. Johnson was, for example, much better than any of his predecessors in teasing out the complex skein of usages which coil around simple words like 'put' and 'make', or almost invisible particles like 'up'. What he called in his *Plan* the 'etymology of phrases' often yields fascinating results, as small words combine to form key parts of English idiom.

The illustrative quotations (there are more than a hundred thousand of them in the first edition) provided a different sort of authority. They built up a kind of encyclopaedic survey of the concerns of the age; Johnson was writing in the period between Ephraim Chambers' *Cyclopaedia* (first published 1728), one of his sources, and the original *Encyclopaedia Britannica* (1768 onwards). As he went about his task, he came to see that a dictionary is not the same thing as an encyclopaedia (he omits entries for proper nouns, found in Bailey and others); nevertheless, as Robert DeMaria has shown, the work did become a map of Johnson's mental universe, as well as an anthology of noble thoughts. He deliberately excluded infidel (atheist) writers, and presented uplifting quotations in such a way as to spread a pervasive message of good living through the text. As we have already noted, the revision in 1773 introduced a further level of moral persuasive and theological exemplum. Beyond all this, the mere citation in bulk of earlier writers helped to define a canon of English classical authors for the first time. Johnson did not go back to Chaucer or Spenser: the standard English he was seeking to describe takes shape in the late sixteenth and seventeenth centuries, and Hooker, Shakespeare, Milton, and Thomas Browne were among the founding fathers. As an indicator of Augustan values in the literature of the seventeenth and eighteenth centuries, the *Dictionary* remains a cultural marker of great interest.

More widely, it was what DeMaria calls a tool for education, and Boswell for one stressed the clarity of mind its definitions promoted, when he broke out with the exclamation that David Hume was but a child in comparison with the great Johnson: 'His *Dictionary* great philosophy; all the axiomatical knowledge of the language; clear ideas.' Johnson would have been pleased with the terms of praise here: he was to write in *Idler* no. 70 a justification for the precise discrimination of shades of meaning which underlay all his lexicographical efforts: 'They that content themselves with general ideas may rest in general terms; but those whose studies or employments force them upon closer inspection, must have names for particular parts, and words by which they may express various modes of combination.' The *Dictionary*, in the end, is a machine for the naming of mental parts; its greatness lies in the finesse with which its author carries out the inventory.

Even if there were no dictionary to go with it, the Preface would be of permanent interest in its own right. Johnson did not succeed perfectly in all the practical tests that were set him by making his book, but he could hardly have had a more lucid sense of what was involved in such an undertaking. It is centrally a review of the causes and effects of change in language, as this is induced by historical, economic, cultural, and geographical factors. Written at the conclusion of his long labours, the Preface not inaptly ends on a personal note, with reflections on a task well performed and a mission (for once, he felt) discharged with honour:

In this work, when it shall be found that much is omitted, let it not be forgotten that much likewise is performed; and though no book was ever spared out of tenderness to the author, and the world is little solicitous to know whence proceeded the faults of that which it condemns; yet it may gratify curiosity to inform it that the *English Dictionary* was written with little assistance of the learned, and without any patronage of the great; not in the soft obscurities of retirement, or under the shelter of academic bowers, but amidst inconvenience and distraction, in sickness and in sorrow: and it may repress the triumph of malignant criticism to observe that if our language is not here fully displayed, I have only failed in an attempt which no human powers have hitherto completed. (W 10. 66)

A man who could use the language with this dignity needs no recommendation from a modern critic to establish his credentials. If dictionary-making guaranteed such a style, we ought all to put some odd hours to making glossaries of our own. Evidently, for Johnson his years on the *Dictionary* had been a formative experience, not just intellectually but morally too.

Speech and writing

Miss Beresford was so much charmed, that she said to me aside, 'How he does talk! Every sentence is an essay.' (B 4. 284).

Johnson lived in an era which highly prized the art of eloquence. Criticism had not yet fully separated itself from rhetoric, and young people were brought up to exercise the skills of composition rather than to analyse them in the work of others. Parliamentary oratory was still regarded as one of the highest modes of discourse, and the budding politician devoted his energies (it was always a he) to the periods of Cicero more often than to the calculations of economists. It was a time when serious adults devoted long hours to mastering 'elocution', which was not then a subject for lisping young misses, as it became in later generations. Thomas Sheridan, father of the dramatist Richard Brinsley, and a man well known to Johnson, moved from the profession of actor to that of teacher of elocution (Boswell attended his lectures in Edinburgh). The role of such a figure embraced those of speech therapist, dialogue coach, theatrical director, and specialist on accents, but the closest modern analogy is perhaps the public-speaking consultant who teaches aspiring public figures how to present their views on television. Allied to this activity was the ambition to codify the speech and gestures of stage actors: it was the dynamic theatrical presence of David Garrick which had inspired this quest, and Garrick himself was interested in the attempt to establish a kind of oral authority. Just as the syntax of a written language points to the way people organize their thinking, so performing style incorporated a syntax of expression. Johnson was alive to the talents of the great comic impersonator, Samuel Foote; and the most popular mode of popular education in the 1760s, 1770s, and 1780s was the so-called 'Lecture on Heads', in which George Alexander Stevens (followed by a host of imitators) anatomized social types in a monologue replete with classical allusions and moral caricatures.

Johnson knew about all these developments, but above all he was bred into a culture which put immense importance on the art of private conversation, another concept with broader implications than it possesses today. Swift and Fielding had each written essays on the subject, seeing the mastery of oral communication as something central to civilized living. Equally, Johnson himself owed much of his contemporary renown to his acknowledged powers in spoken dialogue. Long before the volumes of Johnsoniana or the posthumous biographies transmitted his famous *bons mots*, he had been recognized as supremely good at one of the activities most generally admired in the Hanoverian world. For a long time to come, this aspect of his personality continued to be seen as central, so that writers like Macaulay thought that his conversation would outlive his writings. As late as 1915, a leading authority of the day, C. B. Tinker, wrote that 'posterity is right in preferring Johnson's conversation to his writings, for while it lacks nothing in the stream of thought and finish of style that distinguish his writings, it is distinctly superior in mother wit'. We no longer share the opinion here assigned to posterity, since the literary works have been reclaimed and once more enjoy wide respect. In reaction, there is a risk we shall substitute a facile disdain for the conversation.

Abundant evidence survives to show that Johnson's contemporaries thought his distinction as writer and as speaker proceeded from the same source. A few selected examples will make the point. Fanny Burney wrote that Johnson 'had a facility so complete, that to speak or write produced immediately the same clear and sagacious effect. His pen was as luminous as his tongue, and his tongue was as correct as his pen.' She elsewhere commented on 'how much the same thing it was to hear or to read him' (D&L 1. 120). James Harris remarked that Johnson spoke in such language that a listener would have believed him to be reading, not speaking. Hester Thrale observed that the *Rambler* essays expressed his ideas 'in a style so natural to him, and so like his common mode of conversing' (A 160). The painter Ozias Humphrey stated that everything Johnson said was 'as correct as a second edition' (JM 2. 401). Thomas Tyers agreed: 'his conversation . . . was thought to be equal to his correct writings' (JM 2. 366). His auditors often wished for a written transcript of his conversation: thus, when Boswell deplored the inability of his record to do justice to the 'forcible and brilliant' expression of words pouring forth, a certain Joseph Cradock whispered to him, 'O that his words were written in a book' (B 3. 39). Sir John Hawkins declared that 'his conversational style bore a great resemblance to that of his writings' (H 163). Finally, Sir Joshua Reynolds instanced Johnson as the rare case of a writer who was equally impressive in his conversational powers, indeed regarded by some as superior in this regard (JM 2. 220).

All the individuals quoted knew Johnson well, and their collective testimony can scarcely be controverted at this distance of time. When we are told that Johnson would pick up a topic in social converse and 'utter upon it a number of the *Rambler*' (JM 2. 391), we can hardly suggest that this seems implausible in the light of our own experience. Johnson had taken immense trouble to equip himself; he had trained himself to think in an orderly way and to find suitable expressions to render his ideas; and this applied equally to written and oral communication. Boswell wrote late in life to a friend that Johnson had taught him 'to cross-question in common life', and Reynolds said much the same. There is no reason to suppose that either would have confined this instruction to the written or to the spoken word. The people who spent most time with Johnson, and who imbibed the most from him, are unanimous in their verdict. As modern readers we should be very foolish to try to overset their judgement, to dismiss the 'casual' conversation as mere asides and to reserve our serious attention for the ideas Johnson set down in print.

We can be reasonably sure that the accounts which have come down to us of Johnson in full flow as a talker are reliable in broad outline. It would be pleasant if we could have access to a tape recording or to a transcript by a professional court stenographer, but the gain would be marginal. It is likely that the substance and the manner would not be very different from what we are accustomed to reading. The principal informants, people like Boswell, Fanny Burney, Hester Thrale, Dr John Campbell, and Reynolds, reproduce the same emphases and the same voice. New stories turn up from time to time emanating from stray sources; they seldom, if ever, run counter to the sense we have already acquired of what Johnson sounded like. Of course we do not have in any of these cases a literal word-for-word transcription of the conversation, but the main flow and the spirit have survived. It is not a matter for great concern that Boswell made small marginal alterations from the text of his journal to the printed text of the *Life*: it is entirely plausible that he should have either by research (consulting other people and other sources) or by retrospection have improved on his first memorial reconstruction, to produce a more dependable version.

It is a crucial fact here that none of Johnson's friends complained about the reliability of Boswell's reports. On the contrary, they tended to think that the biographer spilt too many beans. Burke considered that the *Tour to the Hebrides*, for example, divulged too many matters which should have been kept in the realm of private conversation. If the persons best qualified to judge, that is, the circle of Johnson's acquaintance who had heard him perform so often, were disinclined to fault Boswell for accuracy—though they criticized him strongly on many other grounds—it would be comic for a twentieth-century reader to harbour suspicions of grave acts of tampering with the text. Clear evidence is provided by William Walter Pepys, who had known Johnson for many years and was not always uncritical of him, who wrote on the appearance of Boswell's *Tour to the Hebrides*: 'The "Journal" is a most faithful picture of him, so faithful, that I think anybody who has got a clear idea of his person and manner, may know as much of him from that book, as by having been acquainted with him (in the usual way) for three years.' Like Burke, Pepys at the same time deplored the 'indiscretions' of Boswell's narrative, which would make 'sad mischief'. Such indiscretions are dangerous only because they reveal Johnson's true opinions.

We can look, then, at the accounts of the way Johnson spoke as a fair presentation of his characteristic manner. We can see his almost forensic zeal for precision; his typical swoop from particular cases into generalized principles; his wish to deflate cant and humbug; his aim to unmask sophistry and paradox, and to reassert time-honoured wisdom; his relish of fun and his disdain for solemn pedantry. Almost any extended passage in Boswell or Burney will illustrate these characteristics; many of them come through in the dialogues which Reynolds wrote in imitation of his manner. If a single example is required, then the most apt would be, naturally enough, a famous passage in Boswell. This is the meeting with his old college acquaintance Oliver Edwards on Good Friday 1778 after a service at St Clement's Dane. Even such a familiar excerpt comes alive with marvellous freshness when we reread it with care.

Boswell gives 'a pretty full account' of this remarkable encounter (B 3. 302–7). Johnson had just left the service when Edwards 'accosted him with familiar confidence, knowing who he was, while Johnson returned his salutation with a courteous formality, as to a stranger'. In fact Johnson had not immediately recognized one who had been his fellow-student at Pembroke College forty-nine years earlier and whom he had not seen since. Edwards tactlessly blurted out, 'Ah, Sir! we are old men now'. Boswell proceeds:

JOHNSON. (who never like to think of being old,) 'Don't let us discourage one another.' EDWARDS. 'Why, Doctor, you look stout and hearty, I am happy to see you so; for the news papers told us you were very ill.' JOHNSON. 'Ay, Sir, they are always telling lies of *us old fellows*.'

The danger was that the two would now go their separate ways for ever, so Boswell quickly whispered to Edwards that 'he had better accompany' Johnson home while there was a chance of an exchange. The three walked back to Bolt Court, Boswell 'eagerly assisting to keep up the conversation'. Edwards chatted prosily as they went, Johnson apparently absorbed and remaining silent, until a sudden intervention showed the others that he was paying attention to what they said.

When they reached Johnson's house, thanks to Boswell's quiet management, 'the dialogue went on admirably'. Johnson's reserve gradually breaks down, and he quizzes Edwards politely on his life as a lawyer. Then, 'taking himself up all of a sudden', he exclaims: 'O! Mr Edwards! I'll convince you that I recollect you.' He reminds his old acquaintance of their drinking together at an alehouse near the gate of the college. Edwards replies with his immortal *non sequitur*: 'You are a philosopher, Dr Johnson. I have tried in my time to be a philosopher; but, I don't know how, cheerfulness was always breaking in.' Even Johnson can find no immediate response to this extraordinary thought, and the conversation proceeds by fits and starts. With a further onset of tactlessness, Edwards suggests that Johnson has not had the experience of marriage. 'JOHNSON. "Sir, I have known what it was to have a wife, and (in a solemn, tender, faltering tone) I have known what it was to *lose a wife.*—It had almost broke my heart."' Boswell appreciates the moving quality of this admission; Edwards ploughs on regardless. The conversation turns to eating and drinking, with another of Edwards's inimitable thoughts (possibly improved a little by Boswell): 'For my part, now, I consider supper as a turnpike through which one must pass, in order to get to bed.' Again there is no direct response.

By this time Johnson was no doubt growing weary of the exchange, especially when Edwards reverted with fatal ineptitude to the subject of age: 'EDWARDS. "I am grown old: I am sixty-five." JOHNSON. "I shall be sixty-eight next birthday. Come, Sir, drink water, and put in for a hundred."' Even at the moment of leaving, Edwards could not resist another reference:

Mr Edwards, when going away, again recurred to his consciousness of senility, and looking full in Johnson's face, said to him, 'You'll find in Dr Young [Edward Young's *Night Thoughts*], "O my coevals! remnants

77

of yourselves!"' Johnson did not relish this at all; but shook his head with impatience. Edwards walked off, seemingly highly pleased with the honour of having been thus noticed by Dr Johnson.

The two men scarcely ever met again, though once Edwards came upon Johnson and said, 'I am told you have written a very pretty book called *The Rambler*'. Johnson's own account goes on: 'I was unwilling that he should leave the world in total darkness, and sent him a set' (B 4. 90).

For Boswell, 'this interview confirmed my opinion of Johnson's humane and benevolent heart. His cordial and placid behaviour to an old fellow-collegian, a man so different from himself ... showed a kindliness of disposition very rare at an advanced age.' The whole scene, though it was adroitly stage-managed by Boswell, indeed testifies to a capacity in Johnson for openness and sensitivity to others. He was at first puzzled and bored by Edwards; the other man constantly touched on raw nerves, and provoked in Johnson painful memories of his lost wife. Yet there is a truly 'humane' quality in his determination to make something of this strange encounter. This may have been partly out of loyalty to his Oxonian youth, but it also came from his settled resolve to take part in sociable converse so as to receive and impart ideas about the world. Such scenes illustrate qualities in Johnson which are more veiled in his published writings. It is in conversation that we see most clearly the depth of his humanity, not to mention the range of his humour (here kindly held in check, in deference to the solemn self-assurance of Edwards). Humour was a key mode of self-expression for Johnson, and unless we allot it the importance which it generally has in his conversational bouts we shall miss a vital part of his nature.

Immediately after this sequence, Boswell continues his narrative in this way: 'Johnson once observed to me, "Tom Tyers described me the best: 'Sir, (said he), you are like a ghost: you never speak till you are spoken to.'"' (B 3. 307). This is profoundly accurate. Johnson constantly waits for an opening, since his combative attitude towards any conversational adversary made him delay his entrance into an argument until the most effective moment. Fanny Burney describes an evening at her father's house, when the assembled company waited for Johnson to perform, and he resolutely declined to do so. The episode was brilliantly worked up by Virginia Woolf in her sketch, 'Dr Burney's Evening Party', which includes the pregnant observation: 'If there was one thing that Dr Johnson never did, it was to begin.' The trenchancy he displays is more than merely casual aggression; it is rather a sort of cognitive instrument, and one to be to used for the maximum persuasive effect. The natural style of discourse resulting is reactive, sometimes Socratic, dealing not in a priori formulations uttered at large, but in refinements, qualifications, reservations, discriminations. Johnson talked most brilliantly in the company of other brilliant men and women; not surprisingly he valued especially his contests at the Club and elsewhere with Edmund Burke, who 'call[ed] forth all my powers' (B 2. 450). Whilst he never doubted that the foundation of learning must be laid by reading, and that conversation played a supplementary role (B 2. 361), he none the less set high intellectual demands on good conversation. It required knowledge, a command of words, imagination 'to place things in such views as they are not commonly seen in', and presence of mind, so as to be able to think on one's feet (B 4. 166). With cumbrous false modesty, or else curious lack of self-knowledge, he maintained that he lacked the last attribute, and gave up too easily in argument. The truth lies the other way: Johnson, when talking for victory, would go to almost any rhetorical extreme in order to win his case. It was this need to exert all his mental powers on a single limited objective which produced the intensity and vigour of his speech at its most characteristic.

There is no great mystery about the way in which Johnson had sought to achieve the necessary skills. We have his own word for it:

Sir Joshua Reynolds once asked him by what means he had attained his extraordinary accuracy and flow of language. He told him, that he had early laid it down as a fixed rule to do his best on every occasion, and in every company; to impart whatever he knew in the most forcible language he could put it in; and that by constant practice, and never suffering any careless expressions to escape him, or attempting to deliver his thoughts without arranging them in the clearest manner, it became habitual to him. (B 1. 204)

It sounds very simple, put like this. All the same, none of the glittering company who surrounded him—the great orators like

Burke and Fox, the practised rhetoricians like Gibbon, the prominent lawyers like Lord Stowell, smooth men of the world like Joseph Banks, witty socialites like Hester Thrale—quite apart from actors, preachers, ambassadors, courtiers, scholars, and even demagogues like Wilkes—not one of them could regularly match him. By universal consent, he outdid all his contemporaries in the skill and elegance of his conversation.

Johnson is rightly famous for his pithy sayings. A few of these have been spuriously fathered on him, but most are genuine. However, they most often emerge not as detached epigrams in the manner of Oscar Wilde, but as clinching rejoinders or sharp summaries of a wider argument. How much they depend on context for their full weight can be seen by looking at John Buchan's novel *Midwinter* (1923). This has Johnson implausibly involved in the second Jacobite rising (see p. 48 above), twitching and blinking, laying about him with his fists, and perpetually uttering remarks out of the blue along the lines of: 'With you, sir, patriotism is the last refuge of the scoundrel.' Occasionally he paraphrases sections of the *Lives of the Poets* ('Dryden drew from a profundity Pope could not reach'). This turns his thoughtful aperçus into facile pronouncements gushing gratuitously from his lips.

In fact Johnson's maxims take a characteristic form. His sceptical nature led him to doubt the universal truths of confident ideology; on the other hand, his willingness to seek general rules, together with his practice in assembling curt definitions, led him to construct neat experiential formulas. They are what might be called empirical rather than legislative maxims. Moreover, Johnson was not as stiffly resistant to proverbs as was his adversary Lord Chesterfield, and several times, in written and spoken contexts, he uses the form defined in his *Dictionary* as 'a short sentence frequently repeated by the people; a saw; an adage'. Thus he writes to Reynolds in one of his last letters: 'All is not gold that glitters, as we have often been told' (L 3. 230)—the final clause is typical, hinting at possible reservations, but not really withdrawing the substance of the proverb. This is apart from a readiness in applying classical tags which was then the mark of an educated person, and which finds him vying with Burke, Boswell, or Bennet Langton to light on the most apt recollection from ancient literature. Such allusions wear a more serious aspect at times in the printed works; thus Johnson cites the familiar locution *nil mortalibus arduum est* ('nothing is too difficult for mortals to attempt') in his pamphlet on the Falkland Islands, and amplifies it with elegant English variations (Y 10. 358).

Two final tributes are worth quoting because they show the sense people had of Johnson's distinction as a speaker, and how this relates to their expectations of effective written style. The first is from Dr William King, who left it on record that 'Johnson was one of the three men he had known...who spoke English with that elegance and propriety, that if all they said had been immediately committed to writing, any judge of the English language would have pronounced it an excellent and very beautiful style'. The other comes from Edmond Malone, an exacting and highly competent student of these matters: 'Dr Johnson is as correct and elegant in his common conversation as in his writings. He never seems to study either for thoughts or words; and is on all occasions so fluent, so well-informed, so accurate and even eloquent, that I never left his company without regret.'

The Presence of Shakespeare

The work of Shakespeare pervaded Johnson's imagination, from the moment when he read the dramatist 'at a period so early, that the speech of the Ghost in *Hamlet* terrified him when he was alone' (B 1. 70). Whilst on his Scottish tour over half a century later, he strutted about on a heath near Forres, imitating the gestures of Macbeth. In between these dates, he had written *Rambler* papers on topics involving application to Shakespeare; and the plays had been a prime source of illustrative quotations for the *Dictionary*. It would have been difficult for him to avoid the dramatist through all his adult years, since his pupil and lifelong friend David Garrick had presided over a great revival of Shakespeare on the English stage, which was matched by the first great surge in editorial and scholarly work.

Despite their petty rivalries and quarrels, Johnson and Garrick were always close: indeed the friendship with his former student was the longest-lasting contact Johnson maintained, among the people he met regularly on a day-to-day basis. If his friend's death, in Johnson's immortal phrase, 'eclipsed the gaiety of nations', then it also diminished the scope and conviviality of the Johnson circle. Garrick was important to Johnson as a gadfly in Club discussions, as a contact with the working theatre, and as someone willing to try out new textual and dramatic theories in the playhouse. It was Garrick who commissioned and spoke the prologue for Drury Lane in 1747, in which Johnson set out his account of English dramatic history, emphasizing qualities in Shakespeare which were to be endorsed once more in his great Preface to the plays:

> Each change of many-coloured life he drew,
> Exhausted worlds, and then imagined new . . .
> His powerful strokes presiding truth impressed,
> And unresisted passion stormed the breast.
> (Y 6. 87–8)

By this time Johnson had already produced his first specimen of Shakespeare criticism, *Miscellaneous Observations on Macbeth* (1746), in the wake of Garrick's important revival. From that time on Garrick's vigorous campaign on behalf of Shakespeare affected taste in a way which not even the most bigoted and narrow scholar could ignore, and this supplied an essential context for what Johnson wrote.

The second main strand of influence concerns the growth of Shakespearian studies. Here a large contribution was made by Johnson himself, but also by his friends, particularly the editors George Steevens and Edmond Malone. It was a period of lively critical dissent, though often on matters which seem to us to lie some way from the heart of the poetic and dramatic matter. For example, much ink was spilt on the question as to whether or not Shakespeare possessed 'learning', by which was meant knowledge of classical literature. A leading participant in this tiresome debate was Dr Richard Farmer, a good friend of Johnson. More widely, Johnson's concerns naturally brought him into personal contact with an array of literary historians and antiquarians, most of whom worked in the Renaissance period: these included William Oldys, Thomas Birch, Thomas Percy, Thomas Warton, and John Nichols. Independent as he was by nature, and exceptional in his gifts, Johnson can yet be seen to have taken part in a large-scale collaborative enterprise which was going on in his lifetime to set historical scholarship of literature on a sound footing. His work on Shakespeare belongs to a wider movement defined by René Wellek as 'the rise of English literary history'. Like the *Lives of the Poets*, the edition of Shakespeare can be set alongside such undertakings as Thomas Tyrwhitt's work on Chaucer; the debates about Ossian, Chatterton, and (just after Johnson's death) the Shakespeare forgeries of William Henry Ireland; and Malone's researches into Elizabethan drama. Johnson was not a dedicated professional scholar in the manner of some of those named, but he assimilated most of what needed to be known, both as regards factual discoveries and the evolution of scholarly method.

His great edition of Shakespeare (1765) stands at the heart of an impressive attempt to establish the canon and text. The process had begun with Nicholas Rowe in 1709: Rowe's Life remained standard for generations to come. There followed the edition by Pope in 1726, with its thoughtful preface and its idiosyncratic treatment of the text. Lewis Theobald provided a more scholarly and historically aware riposte to Pope in 1734. Hanmer's edition of 1744 is of less moment, although it offered Johnson useful handles for discussion and dissent. Then came William Warburton in 1747, the current standard when Johnson set to work. After Johnson there were Thomas Capell in 1771, George Steevens in 1773, Isaac Reed in 1785, and Malone in 1790: all drew extensively on Johnson. One innovation which his successors took up was the provision of a variorum commentary, embodying the readings and conjectures of earlier editors. In general, the process throughout the century is one of increasing certainty and authority on factual matters—Malone, for example, had a much clearer idea of the order in which the plays were written than his predecessors. On matters of textual transmission there is less by way of unimpeded progress, and Theobald understood this issue as well as anyone who came later. In terms of poetic sensitivity and alertness to linguistic nuance Johnson is rivalled only by Pope; in terms of an overall imaginative response, embodied in notes and preface, Johnson stands alone.

The most complex relationship is that with Warburton. It has recently been argued that Johnson was unduly swayed by some kind words which Warburton had bestowed on the *Observations on Macbeth* in his edition of 1747: 'Johnson's gratitude to Warburton and his prolonged experience of both Warburton and Theobald as editors produced a conflict that continued to influence him'—Peter Seary, *Lewis Theobald and the Editing of Shakespeare* (1990). What happened was that Johnson started off by using Warburton as his copy-text, but in the course of his work came increasingly to rely on Theobald's text. Certainly, Johnson's methods bear more resemblance to the cautious and sceptical ways of Theobald than to the overbearing confidence found in everything that Warburton did. None the less, Johnson possessed the wide general culture and moral convictions of a Warburton, rather than the specialist angle of vision belonging to a vengeful pedant like Theobald. Perhaps the main difference between the two men is that Johnson came to his task in the consciousness of unrewarded merit, if no longer obscure, at least unhounded. Theobald embarked on his edition in the wake of a deep literary trauma, his enthronement as king of the paper-consuming dunces in the original version of Pope's *Dunciad* (1728). Johnson was bent on establishing himself, Theobald on vindicating himself.

In the technical sense, Johnson's performance as an editor is patchy. He had a good grasp of the importance of the First Folio, but he did not use Garrick's library as energetically as he might have done, and his collations are sometimes lazily incomplete. He knew much less about the context of the Elizabethan theatre than Theobald before him and Malone after him. His main advance in narrowly editorial matters proceeds from his reluctance to enter into the competition to produce new readings to supplant allegedly corrupt lines: 'As I practised conjecture more, I learned to trust it less; and after I had printed a few plays, resolved to insert none of my own readings in the text. Upon this caution I now congratulate myself, for every day increases my doubt of my emendations' (Y 7. 108). Assuming that 'the reading is right which requires many words to prove it wrong', Johnson pointed out that the art of the conjectural critic possessed 'no system, no principal and axiomatical truth that regulates subordinate positions', a characteristic statement of the need for rigour and clarity in editorial method—as in any intellectual activity, or so Johnson conceived it. His dry observation: 'the art of writing notes is not of difficult attainment' (Y 7. 108), stands as a rebuke to the more imaginative improvers of Shakespeare's text.

Certain qualities run through all parts of the edition—that is to say, in the Preface, the 'General Observation' at the end of each play, and the explanatory notes scattered throughout the text. One of these is a desire to see Shakespeare straight, to clear away obscurity and cant, and to get back as closely as possible to some unvarnished original meaning. Johnson knew as well as anyone that this presents philosophical difficulties, but he persisted in his effort to bridge the historical gap which led to misunderstandings and misreadings. In his *Proposals* for the edition (1756), he had announced that: 'The business of him that republishes an ancient book is to correct what is corrupt and to explain what is obscure' (Y 7. 51). As we have just seen, Johnson grew less confident as he went about his task regarding the prospects for correcting the corrupt, but he did not waver in his ambition to explain the obscure. The first aspect of this undertaking was to give the contemporary reader glosses on unfamiliar and archaic words, and of course Johnson's experience in compiling the *Dictionary* gave him an advantage here which no previous editor of Shakespeare had enjoyed. The annotation of Johnson's Shakespeare displays a kind of lexicographical precision which extends beyond mere paraphrase of meaning into literary exploration. Thus, when Sir Toby Belch refers in *Twelfth Night* to a knight dubbed 'with unhacked rapier, and with carpet consideration', Johnson launches into a folk-history of the language:

That is, he is no soldier by profession, not a Knight Banneret, dubbed in the field of battle, but, on *carpet consideration*, at a festivity, or on some peaceable occasion, when knights receive their dignity kneeling not on the ground, as in war, but on a carpet. This, I believe, is the original of the contemptuous term a *carpet knight*, who was naturally held in scorn by the men of war. (Y 7. 321)

Johnson did not have to get up an interest in etymology specially for his present task. He had been looking at words critically all his life, especially words used in a literary context, and he enlisted this former intellectual experience in all his scholarly and critical endeavours.

In the passage just quoted from the *Proposals*, Johnson referred to Shakespeare as 'an ancient book'. This was not unrealistic, since a huge chasm had opened up between the sixteenth century and the period of Johnson's lifetime. Comparatively little was known about the day-to-day circumstances of authorship in Shakespeare's time, though scholars were just beginning to investigate the surviving records to build up a more accurate picture of the Elizabethan and Jacobean theatre. But there remained a great watershed of taste, and Johnson naturally felt no more inward affinity with the supplanted ways of writing than did other men and women of his own time. We must remember that there was still no proper history of English literature: Johnson's friend and fellow Clubman Thomas Warton embarked on his *History of Poetry* in 1774, but this work never proceeded beyond the Tudor age, and left no view to compete with Johnson's on (for example) the metaphysical poets. With so much about the past that seemed peculiarly distant and unavailable to the modern mind (a situation produced by the success of Restoration and Augustan campaigns to purify the language of the tribe, and to introduce classical elegance instead of Gothic rawness), it is not surprising that Johnson should have seen his task as one of elucidating an almost foreign text. At every level—from that of the gloss on individual words and phrases, right up to the most general appraisal of Shakespeare's genius—the business of the editor was to strip away the incrustations made by intervening generations, and 'restore' a meaning now lost.

It is for this reason that Johnson begins his Preface with a sounding passage on the 'dignity of an ancient', which could now be claimed by Shakespeare. The impressive opening paragraphs clear the way for an effort to see the dramatist in an historical setting, that is, as a writer situated in a radically different way from a 'modern' author. There is no patronage in this line of approach, though of course bad Augustans could use it to patronize Elizabethans, just as twentieth-century critics can use an inoffensive historicist approach to patronize the treatment of sex by Victorian novelists. By now we have internalized the historical mode of enquiry, and it takes an effort of will to realize that Johnson was labouring in a new and still awkward branch of criticism. The difficulty was compounded by sheer lack of knowledge about conditions in Shakespeare's day. For example, later in the Preface there is a section which greatly exaggerates the chaos amidst which the copy of Shakespeare's plays was transmitted to the press (complicated as that process assuredly was in some cases). But Johnson is making a genuine attempt to come to terms with an epoch whose annals had scarcely been told and whose aesthetic assumptions he can prise out only with the utmost difficulty. Along with the obsolete phraseology of the plays goes a set of obsolete dramatic principles and psychological attitudes, and in each area it is the job of the editor to explain what has become mysterious.

It is in this light that we should read Johnson's bold, if not totally novel, attempt to dispose of the dramatic unities as a necessary guide to the construction of the plays; or his treatment of Shakespeare's sources—the reliance on second-rate romance plots is excused because: 'The English nation, in the time of Shakespeare, was yet struggling to emerge from barbarity' (Y 7. 81), and so popular taste was still undeveloped. A similar awareness lies behind what may seem to us today the most perplexing feature of the Preface, that is, the space devoted to examining the supposed 'faults' of the playwright, faults moreover seen as 'sufficient to obscure and overwhelm any other merit' (Y 7. 71). The fact that Johnson often palliates the fault in question, sometimes by reference to historical considerations, does not palliate the crime for some modern readers. But again we must keep in mind the task as Johnson conceived it—judicial, indeed magisterial; descriptive rather than appreciative; explanatory within a context of imperfect communications with that distant sector of the mental world, the Elizabethan age.

Johnson regularly transcends the ostensible limitations of his position. Sometimes this is because of his independence and clarity of thought:

Shakespeare has united the powers of exciting laughter and sorrow not only in one mind but in one composition. Almost all his plays are divided between serious and ludicrous characters, and, in the successive evolutions of the design, sometimes produce seriousness and sorrow, and sometimes levity and laughter.

That this is a practice contrary to the rules of criticism will be readily allowed; but there is always an appeal open from criticism to nature. The end of writing is to instruct; the end of poetry is to instruct by pleasing.

That the mingled drama may convey all the instruction of tragedy or comedy cannot be denied, because it includes both in its alternations of exhibition and approaches nearer than either to the appearance of life . . . (Y 7. 67)

One can imagine much more complex theoretical justifications of tragicomedy than this (indeed, they have been written), but no more convincing account of why mixed genres can attain their ends.

The key phrase in this passage is 'an appeal open from criticism to nature', and this reminds us that Shakespeare is celebrated in the Preface above all as 'the poet of nature', that is, the writer who 'holds up to his readers a faithful mirror of manners and of life' (Y 7. 62). For Johnson, it is Shakespeare's capacity to tell important truths about the human condition which outweighs any of his defects, real or supposed. His characters are 'the genuine progeny of common humanity, such as the world will always supply, and observation will always find' (Y 7. 62). Romantic bardolatry tended to stress the uniqueness of Shakespeare's creations, fixing on the idiosyncratic, idealized, or psychologically extreme elements of personality which are displayed in the tragedies especially. For Johnson the central human truths reach into much more ordinary areas of living. This difference is partly explained by the changing preoccupations of Augustan and Romantic readers, with their differing ideas about the role of the creative imagination in transforming reality. But the particular quality informing Johnson's Preface, which is equally responsible for the difference, is his warm and responsive feeling for Shakespeare's greatness as the poet of ordinary suffering humanity. It is apt that the finest moment in all his criticism of Shakespeare should occur in a humble note tied to the character, not of a great monarch or tragic hero, but of a weak and depraved comic buffoon: this is from the end-note on *2 Henry IV*:

But Falstaff, unimitated, unimitable Falstaff, how shall I describe thee? Thou compound of sense and vice; of sense which may be admired but not esteemed, of vice which may be despised but hardly detested. Falstaff is a character loaded with faults, and with those faults which naturally produce contempt. He is a thief and a glutton, a coward and a boaster, always ready to cheat the weak and prey upon the poor; to terrify the timorous and insult the defenceless. At once obsequious and malignant, he satirizes in their absence those whom he lives by flattering ... Yet the man thus corrupt, thus despicable, makes himself necessary to the prince who despises him, by the most pleasing of all qualities, perpetual gaiety, by an unfailing power of exciting laughter, which is the more freely indulged as his wit is not of the splendid or ambitious kind but consists in easy escapes and sallies of levity which make no sport but raise no envy. (Y 7. 523)

It is worth noting the familiar terms of address at the start: Johnson has become intimate with Falstaff almost as the knight became intimate with Hal, and through a shared warmth and humour in each case. We might note too that the third sentence in this passage echoes Johnson on Shakespeare's faults (quoted above, p. 87). If Shakespeare is the great dramatist of human interconnectedness, then Johnson is the critic to recognize this. If Shakespeare is the poet of nature, then Johnson is the critic of nature, the man capacious enough intellectually to rethink his standards in the course of formulating his judgement, and wise enough to know that no discourse about human beings can ever be more precise or rule-bound than people themselves are, in their diversity and unpredictability.

The Lives of the Poets

If Johnson had written nothing else, the *Lives of the Poets* (1779–81) would ensure his lasting fame. We still read them with enjoyment, although we have never heard of half of the poets treated and we care little about the critical concepts often invoked. This is a testimony to the quality of the discussion; it does not employ much sophisticated critical technique, as understood today, but it constantly reaches into matters, both human and literary, which do still preoccupy us. The 'lives' are long supplanted as recitals of biographical fact, but they remain shrewd personal appraisals and, in the case of major authors, profound readings of character. Anyone who knows little about, say, Dryden or Pope can turn to Johnson's treatment of these men in the safe knowledge that this is more than a mere 'historic' estimate which has been corrected by subsequent research: in fact, most of the greatest contemporary authorities on both writers revert at frequent intervals to Johnson, for stimulus, suggestion, and renewed insight.

The *Lives* were not intended as a summation of the critical opinions of Samuel Johnson. He harboured no lifelong ambition to produce such a work. It was the booksellers who planned, for commercial reasons, 'an elegant and accurate edition of all the English poets of reputation' (B 3. 110). The plan had been originally to go back as far as Chaucer, but in the event a more orthodox Augustan time-span was imposed, covering writers from the middle of the seventeenth century to the recently dead (no living authors were included; this obviated copyright struggles, but also some delicate editorial decisions). The publishing conglomerate decided at the outset that they wished Johnson to supply prefaces for each individual poet. Terms were agreed—200 guineas for the entire job—and a contract was signed in March 1777. A few weeks later, Johnson wrote to Boswell, 'I am engaged to write little lives, and little prefaces, to a little edition of the English poets' (L 3. 109). The deliberate belittlement of the task may have been less from modesty than from a desire to convince himself that the work would be easily manageable; in the event, it took more time and effort than Johnson could easily summon at the age of 70.

At this point in his letter Johnson added the information that he 'thought [he] had persuaded the booksellers to insert something of Thomson'. It is worth recalling that the selection of poets was essentially out of Johnson's hands, though he was responsible for some four or five additional names. Besides, the choice was unexceptionable by the standards of the age: Johnson would probably have come up with a very similar list himself. Few doubted that the previous one hundred and fifty years had seen the period of outstanding achievement in English poetry. Thomas Warton's *History of English Poetry* was providing a longer perspective, and editors had started to make Chaucer and Spenser more intelligible to the lay reader, even if they were handicapped by what now appear grotesque misunderstandings both of metre and of tone. Johnson's friend Thomas Percy had produced the first great collection of folk ballads (tidied up and bowdlerized, it is true). The practitioners of what was then modernism in literature, such as Gray and Collins, had strained the limits of Augustanism and pointed towards the creation of a new poetic. Indeed, though it is unfashionable to say so, they had opened the way for the

Romantic movement. The collection of English poets to which Johnson contributed the lives was designed to set out the canon as it existed before such revisionism had its effect. Radical editors may project anthologies with polemical intent; publishers generally prefer to assemble what (they know or suspect) the public already relishes.

The structure of most of the individual lives follows a regular plan, falling into three unequal sections. First comes the main biographical treatment, then a general estimate (often quite short), and then a review of the poems in more detail. This is the plan adopted, for example, in the lives of Milton and Pope. In the briefer lives the second section is often truncated, though something of it usually survives, as in the case of Shenstone, where four brief paragraphs describe the subject's private character, his appearance, and outlook ('his mind was not very comprehensive, nor his curiosity active', LOP 3. 354). The proportions are different in the *Life of Savage*, which stands apart from the other items written almost forty years later, and in respect of authors like Roscommon (also written earlier) or Young (mostly the work of another hand). In any case, the divisions are not watertight. The preliminary survey of the writer's career often contains some searching remarks on the works as Johnson proceeds, and the analysis of the poems regularly throws up interesting assessments of the human being behind the text.

In general we find more of substance today in the critical portions. It is true, as we have seen, that Johnson had a long-developed interest in biography, having specialized in this branch of writing during his early years working on the *Gentleman's Magazine*. He retained this interest for the rest of his days. In *Idler* no. 84 he noted: 'Biography is, of the various kinds of narrative writing, that which is most eagerly read, and most easily applied to the purposes of life.' Already in *Rambler* no. 60 he had argued that 'general and rapid narratives of history ... afford few lessons applicable to private life', whereas 'I have often thought that there has rarely passed a life of which a judicious and faithful narrative would not be useful'. Biography, then, was immediately attractive and valuable because its lessons came home to the mass of readers. Here it is worth recalling Johnson's admission, reported by Boswell, that he loved most 'the biographical part of literature' (B 1. 425). It follows that he considered it his duty to perform this part of his task in the 'little prefaces' with a full awareness of their ethical potential: as a memorandum records, they were 'written, I hope, in such a manner as may tend to the promotion of piety' (B 4. 34). But a number of factors have conspired to make the biographical aspect of the work less durable than its critical side.

In the first place, the materials simply did not exist in some cases for a dependable study. Even for the recently dead, Johnson often had to rely on casual anecdotes and second-hand gossip. Where there was no full-scale biography already published, as is true of most of the minor writers, he was obliged to fall back on collective works of reference, such as the series of lives attributed to Theophilus Cibber, and they rarely contained much of value. In the strictest sense, all the items can be regarded as 'derivative' with the exception of Savage, although this does not mean that they are worthless. In the big lives, notably those of Milton, Dryden, and Pope, we can easily discern that Johnson has reappraised the evidence and put his own stamp on the material. This applies even to the study of Swift, although it has been shown that Johnson follows very closely, paragraph by paragraph, the biography of his friend John Hawkesworth which had appeared in 1755. In fact, Hawkesworth's treatment contains more fresh 'research', as we should look for that in a modern biographer, but anyone seeking a radical reconsideration of Swift's personality will find much more to chew on in Johnson's coverage. In this particular case it is odd to find the rapid concluding dismissal of the verse ('In the poetical works of Swift there is not much upon which the critic can exercise his powers', LOP 3. 65), but it must be remembered that the rediscovery of Swift as a major poet is almost entirely a phenomenon of the twentieth century.

The truth is that Johnson did not have the instincts of a research scholar, in the sense of a single-minded enquirer carrying out intensive studies in a narrow area. His mind was too inclusive, too readily drawn to general reflection, too impatient of trivial detail. By this time in his own life, he was reluctant to perform the kind of endless running around which enabled Boswell to check on long-forgotten facts. He still valued the moral force of biography, but he had lost whatever urge he had ever had to root about in dusty archives—and there were fewer such archives available than there would be later. What Johnson seeks fundamentally is a mental construct of the man in question, and events are utilized to build up this portrait, rather than to establish a definitive life-history. I use the word 'man' with strict accuracy, since all the poets in the collection were male. Forty years later Walter Scott would admit a few female authors to the *Lives of the Novelists*, and today we should have no trouble in finding women poets we should want to include among the more interesting of the seventeenth and eighteenth centuries; but the booksellers were not being eccentric in leaving out authors such as Lady Winchilsea or the Duchess of Newcastle, who still occupied a special protected niche which ruled out serious assessment of their work on the same footing as that of men.

Any limitations of the *Lives* as biography are of secondary importance, since we turn to them these days chiefly for their profound critical coverage. Johnson's standards are those of an earlier age, and his emphases lie differently from those which most readers would find natural in the wake of romanticism and modernism. To speak broadly, his critical positives include freshness, truth to nature, vigour, clarity, energy, sharpness of focus, and wit. It is perhaps easier to start with defining by negatives. The attributes Johnson disliked in the poets he discussed included triteness, staleness, affectation, over-ingenuity, and perverseness (the habit of rooting around for paradox, once more). He opposes hereditary images, inert conventionalities of thought and diction, avoidance of the natural. When he locates 'nature', then that means something like 'the nature of things', a realistic representation of what is commonly to be found. He also has a particular objection to archaism—Collins 'affected the obsolete when it was not worthy of revival, and he put his words out of the common order, seeming to think . . . that not to write prose is certainly to write poetry' (LOP 3. 341). The much-discussed attack on *Lycidas* contains the assertions:

In this poem there is no nature, for there is no truth; there is no art, for there is nothing new. Its form is that of the pastoral . . . whatever images it can supply are long ago exhausted, and its inherent improbability always forces dissatisfaction on the mind . . . With these trifling fictions are mingled the most awful and sacred truths, such as ought never to be polluted with such irreverent combinations. (LOP 1. 165)

For Johnson, religious poetry was in itself a difficult issue, and to find devotional material mixed in with the tired platitudes of a pagan form was doubly disagreeable.

It should be added that some of the touchstones which Johnson uses are more narrowly aesthetic: he looks for order and design in poetry, and accordingly marks down Thomson's *Seasons* on account of their 'want of method'—of the varied topics taken up in this poem 'no rule can be given why one should be mentioned before another; yet the memory wants the help of order, and the curiosity is not excited by suspense or expectation' (LOP 3. 300). In other words, the poet risks boring us, since the developing drama which draws us along in reading a narrative or a logically designed argument is absent. And nothing could compensate for a lack of interest; all literary virtues were useless without this. 'Tediousness', he observes in the life of Prior, 'is the most fatal of all faults; negligences or errors are single and local, but tediousness pervades the whole: other faults are censured and forgotten, but the power of tediousness propagates itself' (LOP 2. 206). Happily this is a power absent from the *Lives of the Poets*.

The comment on Thomson illustrates a desire on Johnson's part to go back to first principles. This characteristic is also visible in the Life of Cowley, where Johnson provides his finest piece of sustained critical analysis as he anatomizes the wit of Donne and his followers—this remains one of the most observant and penetrating readings of the metaphysical style which has ever been written:

Nor was the sublime more within their reach than the pathetic; for they never attempted that comprehension and expanse of thought which at once fills the whole mind, and of which the first effect is sudden astonishment, and the second rational admiration. Sublimity is produced by aggregation, and littleness by dispersion. Great thoughts are always general, and consist in positions not limited by exceptions, and in descriptions not descending to minuteness. It is with great propriety that subtlety, which in its original import means exility of particles, is taken in its metaphorical meaning for nicety of distinction. Those writers who lay on the watch for novelty could have little hope of greatness; for great things cannot have escaped former observation. Their attempts were always analytic: they broke every image into fragments, and could no more represent by their slender conceits and laboured particularities the prospects of nature or the scenes of life, than he who dissects a sunbeam with a prism can exhibit the wide effulgence of a summer noon. (LOP 1. 20–1)

Few modern admirers of the metaphysical poets will accept this argument as a whole, but no one can deny the clarity and vigour of the reasoning. It is much the same when Johnson addresses *Paradise Lost*: in particular, his preliminary assessment of the work as epic, according to the strict expectations which were then brought to the highest of all literary genres, defines the artistic grandeur of the undertaking with superb precision. Whatever reservations Johnson may have had about aspects of Milton's personality, along with his political views, there is nothing half-hearted about the account of *Paradise Lost*, in the loftiness of its aim and the majesty of its execution.

A thread running through all the *Lives* is Johnson's belief in the general applicability of great poetry. He shared the prevailing opinion of his era that 'poetry has to do rather with the passions of men, which are uniform, than their customs, which are variable' (*Rambler* no. 36). Since human nature is fundamentally uniform, literature at its most effective deals with recurring and readily identifiable states of existence; poets such as Milton, Dryden, and Pope—unlike the metaphysicals—confront what is central, and not what is aberrant. Good writing is widely applicable; it is not limited to the special circumstances of an individual author. Of course, Johnson recognized that poetry also dealt with intense moments of vision and vivid apprehension of sharply observed detail. The point is that the major writer will give these moments and these details a meaning that transcends the local occasion. By selection and emphasis, Milton was able to invest a wide range of materials with a general significance:

Here is a full display of the united force of study and genius; of a great accumulation of materials, with judgement to digest and fancy to combine them: Milton was able to select from nature or from story, from ancient fable or from modern science, whatever could illustrate or adorn his thoughts. An accumulation of knowledge impregnated his mind, fermented by study and exalted by imagination.

It has been therefore said without an indecent hyperbole by one of his encomiasts, that in reading *Paradise Lost* we read a book of universal knowledge. (LOP 1. 183)

In conclusion, it needs to be stressed that Johnson values literature ultimately for its relation to life—the illumination it cast on our experience, and the power it has to make us live more fully. He insisted that we need 'to see things as they are' (L 1. 111), and it was a prime function of literature to assist in this process. 'The only end of writing is to enable the readers better to enjoy life, or better to endure it' (W 12. 301). Like all branches of human enquiry, literature is the servant of a higher activity, that is, morality. The *Lives* serve as a species of conduct book, weighing the contribution of different poets to this great task; the fuller their report on human experience, the more substantial will be their literary achievement, and the more lasting their endowment to the common stock of human good.

7 Time and place

Johnson's greatest poem, *The Vanity of Human Wishes*, begins with a sweeping gesture indicating the scope of its ambition: 'Let observation with extensive view,|Survey mankind, from China to Peru...' This prepares the reader for an anatomy of human experience to be conducted in spatial terms, with the diversity of life imaged by geographical markers. In the event, the poem is organized much more along historical lines. Almost the same thing happens in a work by Johnson's great friend Goldsmith, *The Traveller* (1764), where again the poem swings from a vision of Europe spread out before the traveller into a survey of the history of peoples. Neither Johnson nor Goldsmith is really veering away from the subject in hand. There was then a close alliance in education between history and geography. Much of Gibbon's formative reading took the form of itineraries, topographic and chorographic accounts, atlases and gazetteers. Johnson's interest in place has been more widely appreciated than his sense of the past, partly because his own *Journey to the Western Islands* holds an imperishable place of honour in the literature of travel. We need, however, to do justice to the other dimension in this pairing.

Travel

By the standards of his day, Johnson was not peculiarly obsessed by travel. He lived in a period when exploration and discovery opened up a wider world, and when internal communications improved so as to make domestic travel more quick and convenient. Everyone felt the impress of these developments: Johnson registers some of the changing attitudes which resulted, but this is because he was a great writer fully alive to his own era, rather than because he devoted special attention to the topic. As an avid reader, he could not miss the explosive growth in collections of voyages and other travel narratives, which contributed amongst other things to the way the early novel evolved. It is this background of armchair travel which underlies the exotic fiction of *Rasselas*; a pervasive 'journey motif' has been discovered in the *Rambler*, and this could be seen as the adaptation of an ancestral image in the light of the new implications of such an image when literal journeying had developed in such momentous ways.

Johnson had a clear idea of the benefits of travel and its limitations. He expected from the seasoned traveller a particularly close report of empirical facts, that is, an extension of the reader's experience made possible by the writer's contact with a larger reality. It was an expectation often to be dashed, as *Idler* no. 97 reveals: 'The greater part of travellers tell us nothing, because their method of travelling supplies them with nothing to be told.' The paper goes on to consider the reasons why 'few books disappoint their readers more than the narrations of travellers'. A representative flaw is that of confining attention to the surface of the landscape:

Those who sit idly at home, and are curious to know what is done or suffered in distant countries, may be informed by one of these wanderers, that on a certain day he set out early with the caravan, and in the first hour's march saw, towards the south, a hill covered with trees, then passed over a stream, which ran northward with a swift course, but which is probably dry in the summer months; that an hour after he saw something to the right which looked at a distance like a castle with towers, but which he discovered afterwards to be a craggy rock . . .

And so on for twenty more lines: 'Thus he conducts his reader through wet and dry, over rough and smooth, without incidents, without reflection.' Here the redundancy of detail is beautifully caught in phrases such as 'something to the right'. Johnson was enough of a Baconian to want the external world properly charted and described, but this was not sufficient: there had to be 'incident', that is, human contact or reaction, and 'reflection'. In a letter to Hester Thrale, whilst on his Scottish trip, Johnson wrote that 'the use of travelling is to regulate imagination by reality, and instead of thinking how things may be, to see them as they are' (L 1. 359). To see things as they are is not just inertly to take snapshots along the way, but to process the experiential data by means of mental reappraisal and reflection.

As it happened, Johnson's first major prose work was itself a translation from the French of a travel book, the *Voyage to Abyssinia* by a seventeenth-century Portuguese Jesuit missionary. Johnson toned down the Catholic import of the work but otherwise produced a reasonably faithful translation. Some of the material stayed in his head when, two decades later, he chose Abyssinia as the site of the Happy Valley in *Rasselas*: a more potent expressive sign in the philosophic tale is, however, the River Nile itself, which for centuries had been used as a symbol of the mysterious and tantalizing (its source was, of course, still unknown). The inundation of the Nile marks the denouement of a tale which confessedly has no denouement as far as the characters are concerned; it is as though the great natural forces of immemorial nature have asserted their indifference to the puny aspirations of human beings. Since the flooding of the Nile had shaped so much of the history of one of the greatest civilizations of the world, Johnson is dealing with far more than arid geographical fact. He uses his oriental setting, not playfully, as does Voltaire in such works as *La Princesse de Babylon*, or for the purposes of bluff and evasion, as does Beckford in *Vathek*; for Johnson the oriental tale was a useful conventional framework in which he could explore large issues without the constraints of the familiar and the distractingly particular. The Happy Valley is generalized, if not quite mythic, whereas the Thames Valley would have been uncomfortably precise and referential.

Johnson led a fairly statuesque existence. Apart from occasional trips to places like Oxford and Derbyshire, he rarely strayed far from London in his middle years. It was something of a surprise to his acquaintances that in his sixties he should have ventured with Boswell to the Hebrides, and with the Thrales to North Wales and then to Paris. It is true that Johnson was sometimes comically out of his element in the wilds of Scotland—but that, as we shall see in a moment, was part of the reason for going there. In fact, as Mrs Thrale discovered, again somewhat against expectation: 'Johnson was in some respects a very good travelling companion: the rain, and the sun, the night and the day were the same to him, and he had no care about food, hours or accommodations.' Honesty compels us to pursue this quotation into its sequel: 'But then he expected that nobody else should have any either, and felt no sort of compassion for one's fatigue, or uneasiness, or confinement in the carriage' (T 1. 187). The signs are that Johnson would have been a more regular traveller if circumstances had permitted. To the end of his days he harboured the desire for a sight of the Great Wall of China.

His trips with the Thrales yielded only minor recitals of fairly inconsequential detail. But his one sustained journey into the unknown, the Hebridean jaunt, produced one of the most searching encounters with an alien culture which any writer has ever brought before the world. There is the added bonus that the same trip yielded a book of remarkable interest by Boswell: a more shallow and personalized account, it is true, but one which points up the depth of Johnson's response to the Highlands and Islands by the vividly commonplace nature of its own report on the same events.

There are two important contexts in which we must seek to interpret the element of travel in *A Journey to the Western Islands*. The first is the background of exploration in the previous decade, culminating in James Cook's first voyage of 1768–71. No sentient being could have been unaware of the national interest generated by Cook's expeditions: his discoveries effected a Copernican revolution in the Western sense of the shape of the world, the 'great map of mankind' to which Burke referred. Together with the explorations of men like Wallis and Bougainville, the Cook voyages supplied a new geography and a new anthropology: the ideas of Rousseau were suddenly transferred from theoretical models in the laboratory to a human testing-ground. But there is no need to rely on such general influence. Johnson met Joseph Banks and Daniel Solander, the principal scientist on the first voyage, when they returned to England with Cook. Then again, Johnson's friend and successor on the *Gentleman's Magazine*, John Hawkesworth, wrote the official account of the voyages for a ready market of book-buyers. There are abundant signs that Johnson was keenly aware of the mania for exploration when he set out with Boswell for the Western Islands. His book is necessarily in some part a Cook's voyage on the European scale: it is an encounter with a people still savage in some technical respects, as remote from Johnson's habitual experience as Botany Bay was for Cook's party. Moreover, Johnson had in mind the published travel books of his acquaintance Baretti and the musical tours of his friend Charles Burney (published 1771–3), and borrowed some particular tricks of layout and presentation from these two sources. A more pervasive debt is to the spirit of cross-cultural comparison which journeys like that of Cook had brought into notice. Plainly Johnson was on the lookout in Scotland for curiosities, natural and human, to match the travellers' tales he had heard from Banks, who would soon be elected to the Literary Club. It was, we recall, on this excursion into Caledonia that Johnson gave his famous impersonation of a kangaroo, whose existence had been reliably reported for the first time by Banks and his artists.

The second context is that of aristocratic travel on the continent, an experience valued by Johnson but denied to him by his lack of means. As late as 1776 he still harboured some hopes of venturing as far as the Mediterranean, as Boswell records:

A journey to Italy was still in his thoughts. He said, 'A man who has not been in Italy, is always conscious of an inferiority, from his not having seen what it is expected a man should see. The grand object of travelling is to see the shores of the Mediterranean. On these shores were the four great Empires of the world: the Assyrian, the Persian, the Grecian, and the Roman.—All our religion, almost all our law, almost all our arts, almost all that sets us above the savages, has come to us from the shores of the Mediterranean.' (B 3. 36)

One could argue that Johnson did pretty well without the advantages of a Mediterranean trip, and that he managed to cope with the sense of 'inferiority' this should have bred. But he continued to hanker after Italy to the end of his life, even though he was fully aware that Grand Tourists were often too grand in their ways to get much serious educational benefit from their time abroad.

In fact the Hebridean jaunt was many things—a pleasure trip, a half-guilty entry into the land he had often reviled, a break from London, and as we have just seen, a replication on the domestic scale of a Pacific expedition. But its most central aspect can be described as that of a Grand Detour, that is to say, a mirror-image of the conventional Grand Tour. Normally such journeys were undertaken by the young and well-heeled: Johnson was elderly and poor. The tourists went south, to the cradle of European civilization; Johnson went to the north, where vestiges of earlier generations were sparse. They sought out bookish surroundings, classic ground where every footstep might bring a line of Virgil or Horace to mind; Johnson went to the home of a pre-literate culture, where oral transmission had to perform, inefficiently, the tasks easily handled by the legatees of ancient Rome. Tourists habitually spent most of their time in cities, attended plays, concerts, and galleries, and met others of their class and background at social gatherings. By contrast, Johnson and Boswell never found a town after Inverness until they arrived at Glasgow many weeks later; they moved among small, isolated communities, and met very few people from their own world. Finally, the Grand Tour carried the attractions of a sojourn in a warm climate, amid comfort, luxury, and licensed profligacy. The road to the isles involved for Johnson cold, danger at sea, and a whole environment of penury and repressed conformity. In all these respects the trip involved a flight from traditional Grand Tour norms; unable to join the privileged travellers, Johnson decided to beat them by inventing an educational journey radically opposite in geographical drift and in cultural valency.

As soon as Johnson leaves Edinburgh (significantly he regards this as 'a city too well known to admit description' (Y 9. 3)—in terms of the dialectic just laid out, *any* city would have been outside the plan), the nature of his undertaking becomes clear. There are major stopping-points such as St Andrews and Aberdeen *en route*, but a steady pull is felt towards the wild and remote. The theme of the book fully announces itself as Johnson reaches the Highlands proper, which were then still scarcely within the remit of Westminster law as the clan system withered in the wake of Culloden. It is indicative that a prolonged analytic section is kept until the travellers have arrived on Skye. They were trapped there for a time as bad weather forbad sailing to the other islands. At this juncture Johnson launches into his most sustained piece of social and historical analysis. The topics under review include enforced emigration, chiefly to America; the so-called 'second sight' or gift of paranormal perception; the system of tacksmen or agents between landlord and tenant; and the validity of James Macpherson's claim to have uncovered an ancient bard called Ossian.

Perhaps the subject right at the heart of the book, however, is the general issue of oral culture: what it is, what it can and cannot preserve, what it implies for the people who live by its dictates. Sceptically, Johnson observes that where other Celtic languages such as Welsh have produced a notable literary tradition, in the Highlands there was no such Gaelic legacy: 'the Earse merely floated in the breath of the people.' In a bookish culture,

By degrees one age improves upon another. Exactness is first obtained, and afterwards elegance. But diction, merely vocal, is always in its childhood. As no man leaves his eloquence behind him, the new generations have all to learn. There may possibly be books without a polished language, but there can be no polished language without books. (Y 9. 115–16)

It is possible to disagree with Johnson here, in the light of modern studies of primitive society, but one cannot fail to admire his powers of observation and description, his ability to marshal facts, and his readiness to enter into the texture of the lives he has come to inspect. Every Augustan generality here ('exactness', 'polite') has a concrete meaning for Johnson; and his capacity to diagnose an overall condition among the Highland people derives from his willingness to look and listen. He knew that he would be an oddity in the wild places, an Englishman in his sixties who had spent most of his life in the metropolis; but he did not shirk from the human engagement this was bound to promote, awkward and embarrassing as it might be.

An abiding impression of the book for most readers will be Johnson the intrepid traveller: not just physically adventurous (though he was certainly that, to embark on such a long slog in difficult terrain, at his time of life), but in his mental preparedness. Boswell was astonished to see his friend transported to these unlikely climes; but it is wholly characteristic of Johnson that he should put himself to the test. There is in him a wild, untamed, Caliban-like quality, and unlike the refined Grand Tourist he never sets himself above the people he meets on his peregrination. Later he once described the experience to Boswell as a 'frolic' (B 4. 136), but this understates the arduousness of the trip, and not surprisingly he did not wish to repeat the experiment: 'Other people may go and see the Hebrides.' The last word on the journey occurs in a conversation ten years on, not much more than eighteen months before his death: 'I got an acquisition of more ideas by it than by anything that I remember. I saw quite a different system of life' (B 4. 199). Like Cook, Johnson had sailed towards new continents of thought: he had used his travels, as he had always envisaged the matter, to acquire new ideas.

The point of the trip was also to confront old ideas in fresh surroundings. The Highlands were still untamed: as Johnson wrote back to Mrs Thrale, 'I have now the pleasure of going where nobody goes, and of seeing what nobody sees' (L 1. 338). On his return he told his friend John Taylor, 'I have seen a new region' (L 1. 393). It was a human inquiry rather than a geographical or antiquarian survey: as the prince observes in *Rasselas*: 'My curiosity does not very strongly lead me to survey piles of stone, or mounds of earth; my business is with man' (Y 16. 111). The journey made a deep impression on Johnson's mind, and he often adverted to his Hebridean experiences over the last few years of his life. He more than once told Boswell that 'the time spent in this tour was the pleasantest part of his life' (B 5. 405). This might seem surprising in view of the rigours he underwent, but it was a great learning experience, and Johnson always wished to improve his understanding of life.

There were assuredly some personal feelings bound up in his decision to take the trip: he may have been working out some of his lifelong anxieties as he traversed this remote and empty landscape. It was a dose of reality, after the habituating and sometimes dulling routine of London existence. It was a way of testing the theories that had grown up around primitive culture, by observing a 'savage' society (as it might be called in strict technical terms at this date): 'description is always fallacious, at least till you have seen realities' (L 3. 69). Finally, the act of composing the *Journey* was itself designed to meet a challenge, for as we have seen, Johnson held a low opinion of most previous travel writing. 'Those whose lot is to ramble can seldom write', he told Mrs Thrale, 'and those who know how to write very seldom ramble' (L 1. 243). His own book is a triumphant demonstration that this depressing state of affairs could be changed.

> The study of *chronology* and *history* seems to be one
> of the most natural delights of the human mind. It is
> not easy to live without enquiring by what means
> everything was brought into the state in which we
> now behold it. (W 10. 295)

It is a piquant thought that Johnson might have been a great
historian—perhaps ought to have been. He had all the
requirements. Intellectually he was well suited to the task. 'No
man better understood the nature of historical evidence than Dr
Johnson', wrote Arthur Murphy; 'no man was more religiously an
observer of truth' (JM 1. 479). His well-known contention that
'distrust is a necessary qualification of a student in history' (W 11.
219) points to his own habitual scepticism. It is no accident that
Johnson interested himself in a dispute about certain alleged
plagiarisms in Milton's work, an allegation disproved by John
Douglas, later a member of the Club; and that he vehemently
opposed the claims of originality for the so-called works of
Ossian, published by James Macpherson. When he went to Bristol
in 1776 he immediately conducted his own inquiry into the
'authenticity' of Chatterton's poems, emerging, in Boswell's
words, 'quite satisfied of the imposture, which, indeed, has been
clearly demonstrated from internal evidence, by several able
critics' (B 3. 50). One of his missions in life was to expose frauds,
as in the case of the alleged Cock Lane Ghost in 1762.

Johnson's abundant reading had equally fitted him for the study
of history. His researches in ecclesiastical and theological
matters, his love of geography, his lexicographical and editorial
work, his taste for biography, and much else—all show the
impress of historical issues upon his mind. The *Dictionary*, for
example, is stuffed with historical quotations; the linguistic
preparation Johnson undertook led him to read the Saxon scholars
who were opening up the formerly dark ages of earlier English
culture. He supported the work of one such scholar, Edward Lye.
In his edition of Shakespeare he attempted to set the dramatist in
his Elizabethan context more fully than had been done before. His
notes make use of chroniclers like Holinshed and historiographers
(or myth-makers) like Geoffrey of Monmouth. He reviewed

several works of history when writing for the literary journals, and devoted periodical papers to the subject. When he went to the Hebrides he read the standard history before leaving England. His work on the Vinerian Law Lectures involved him in considering the origins of common law and therefore the political and social conditions of medieval England. His *Lives of the Poets* allowed him to unload a mass of incidental information which he had acquired over the years concerning the literary history of the nation.

It is no surprise, then, to learn that almost a quarter of the books in his library can be identified as belonging to the sphere of history—ancient, medieval, Renaissance, or modern. He had, after all, helped to compile the great catalogue of the Harleian Library (1744), which carried with it the labour of sorting through thousands of books of antiquarian interest. He had grown up in a bookshop, whose clientele included the Lichfield clergy, with their inclination towards works of scholarship. He had briefly studied at Oxford, the site of much of the finest antiquarian research in this era, with pioneers in almost every branch of historical enquiry. He regularly visited castles and cathedrals, and in Scotland spent much of his time meditating upon the ruins he came across. His friends included several important antiquarian scholars and historians.

Yet, in spite of all this, he never composed a full-dress work of major history. He started but abandoned a life of Paolo Sarpi, one of the greatest of Renaissance historians. He projected a number of other books in this department of learning, of which the most interesting might have been a history of 'the revival of learning in Europe' (B 4. 382) and a design of translating Thuanus, that is, the sixteenth-century historian Jacques-Auguste de Thou (B 4. 410). Something blocked or averted these plans. Despite his massive qualifications, Johnson wrote no more than sketches, brief reviews, prolegomena. Moreover, he expressed considerable reservations at times concerning the worth of much history as it was actually written. Some of these testy comments can be put down to religious factors, such as his dislike of Gibbon and Hume as exponents of infidelity; others may be playful and provocative. Nevertheless, we cannot sweep aside all these negative comments. In the end Johnson did not feel called to give the world the great work of history of which he was capable; and—highly significant, for one of his temper—he did not express any guilt on that score.

Some branches of historical writing elicited his profound respect: informative biography was one, literary history another, and we may deduce from *Rasselas* that he shared the views of Imlac in chapter 30, to the effect that: 'There is no part of history so generally useful as that which relates the progress of the human mind, the gradual improvement of reason, the successive advances of science, the vicissitudes of learning and ignorance ... the extinction and resuscitation of arts, and all the revolutions of the intellectual world' (Y 16. 113). Indeed, he seems to endorse everything Imlac says in this context, including the well-known statement that: 'To judge rightly of the present we must oppose it to the past.' Clearly Johnson cannot have regarded all concern with bygone times as mere antiquarian footling. His own map of learning, quite apart from his practice as a writer, would preclude such a conclusion.

Still, he found a great deal to disparage. Trivial listing of detail for the sake of it would lack the moral and human seriousness he always sought; so he spoke of the spirit of history as 'contrary to minuteness' (B 1. 155), and compared a modern historian unfavourably with a modern moralist, as 'there is but a shallow stream of thought in history' (B 2. 195). He disliked conjectural and romanticized history, insisting that it was necessary to remember 'how very little real history there is: I mean real authentic history' (B 2. 365). Yet at the same time he was able to praise the laborious annals of Lord Hailes, and to keep a fondness for the slanted high-Tory history of Thomas Carte. He criticized the verbosity of William Robertson, but found much to admire in a different brand of social and cultural historian, that is, Voltaire, whose *Essai sur les mœurs* perhaps best exemplifies the account of 'the progress of the human mind' Imlac had called for. Political and national factors sometimes intervened, so that his judgement of works deriving from the Edinburgh illuminati may have been adversely affected. But he was also short with the radical historian Catherine Macaulay on grounds that seem to be other than literary. Johnson brought the whole cluster of his preferences and prejudices to the assessment of any work of historiography, and we should not too readily assign his judgements to a coherent theory of the subject.

Modern scholars have concluded that Johnson knew much more about the practice of history than has generally been thought, and that historical enquiry played a large part in his entire intellectual scheme of things. We still have to deal, though, with his disconcerting reservations—his conviction, for example, that: 'Great abilities are not requisite for an historian ... Imagination is not required in any high degree' (B 1. 424). Again, Johnson observed in his Life of Dryden that: 'To adjust the minute events of literary history is tedious and troublesome; it requires indeed no great force of understanding' (LOP 1. 368). There is a subtle shift here, so that we are inclined to think that what is tedious and troublesome to write must also be tedious and troublesome to read—an effect Johnson may have intended to create. Then there is his famous, if not notorious, injunction to Hester Thrale: 'Wherever you are and whatever you see talk not of the Punic War' (L 2. 57). Sportive as the tone is, Johnson meant what he said at some level. We could argue that he pointed to bad historical writing (mindless, unnecessarily detailed, morally unconcerned), and was not dismissing the entire enterprise. Quite so; but why did bad writing appear, in his view, so often in such a context? In some subterranean cranny of his personality Johnson was acutely disturbed by the faults of the historian, more than by parallel deficiencies in those who practised other genres. This could even be a reflex of his own failure to deliver that of which he was so manifestly capable himself. 'The first qualification of a writer', *Adventurer* no. 115 informs us, 'is a perfect knowledge of the subject which he undertakes to treat.' Johnson could not easily have relinquished the role of historian to the incompetent and the unlearned. There are still puzzles and problems here.

8 Conclusion

'His trade was wisdom', said Giuseppe Baretti, who knew Johnson as well as most. Whether we are considering *The Vanity of Human Wishes*, or the *Rambler*, or *Rasselas*, or for that matter the conversations, this comment will stand. We value the best of the criticism, in the Preface to Shakespeare, or the Lives of Milton or Pope, not because of its innovative methods of analysis or any unique aesthetic insight, but because of its sense of the human in literature—an awareness of profound constants in all the varied moods and mutations of the different lives which individuals lead. Johnson observed of Shakespeare: 'His persons act and speak by the influence of those general passions and principles are agitated, and the whole system of life is continued in motion' (Y 7. 62). Art at its highest reproduces not abnormal or aberrant experience, but the most representative sensations and perceptions which may be felt by all of us. This stress on common experience makes it possible for general deductions to be drawn and (for working purposes) permanent conclusions reached. Nowadays we are inclined to regard life as a more fragmentary business, and literature tends to be engaged with the fleeting, the personal and inchoate. Born into a more robust culture, and possessed of specially solid habits of reasoning, Johnson was able to declare himself more confidently on matters of general observation, to survey mankind across the sweep of time and place, and to deliver the words of the sage.

The amazing thing is that the longer we look at Johnson's apparent platitudes, the less platitudinous they seem. A century after Johnson, as already remarked, Taine could assert that 'ses vérités sont trop vraies'. That now has a very dated air: we are more willing to uncover the process by which Johnson arrived at his certainties, the struggle underlying his qualified hope, the wide-ranging scrutiny of possibilities which explains his brave pessimism, and the compassionate sense of human frailty which still permits his most austere judgements on cruelty or complacence. We have learnt not to mistake his fierce orthodoxy in many areas for unthinking conformism, or to misread his loyal Tory sentiments as the reflexes of a backwoods reactionary. Above all, we have learnt never to underrate the element of passion in his overtly rational world-view. Johnson's contemporaries knew well enough that his intellectual life had embodied a constant warring with strong drives and potentially destructive traits; today we are even more aware of the strength of character which was required for Johnson to reach the personal authenticity and public authority he achieved.

In fact, some of the best pointers to the nature of this achievement can be found in the comments of those who knew Johnson the man. The learned Elizabeth Carter wrote on his death of 'the irritations of a most suffering state of nervous constitution': she was addressing Mrs Elizabeth Montagu, who had quarrelled with Johnson, and Mrs Carter would not have palliated Johnson's faults unduly. Another prominent woman of letters, Lady Craven, stated: 'Gigantic and extraordinary as his thoughts and language were, there was a goodness of heart that pierced through all his learning.' Hester Thrale, who was permitted to see more of Johnson's inner torments than any other living being, later observed: 'He preferred veracity to interest, affection, or resentment, nor suffered partiality or prejudice to warp him from the truth.' Many came to value his sturdy advice: often this took the form used to the painter's sister, Frances Reynolds: 'Ponder no more, Renny, whatever you do, do it, but ponder no more!' Even those who disagreed with his political or theological views appreciated the bracing quality of his moral outlook: witness the Orientalist Sir William Jones: 'Dr Johnson's advice (and though I dislike his principles, I venerate his intellect) is this: "*Persist*: for if you lose the election, you will gain considerable honour by *having stood*".' Johnson went on standing, and gained honour with those around him by what might be called his principled resolution. The fortitude of a death he feared simply confirmed a quality of heroism apparent in all his life and work.

If an already impressive life can be ennobled still further by death, then the story of Johnson's last days must exemplify such a case. Perhaps his most characteristic single remark is one Boswell quotes from a few weeks before the end: 'I will be conquered; I will not capitulate' (B 4. 374). The statement contrives to blend stern resolution with ultimate serenity and resignation. It gains its force from our knowledge that Johnson had always been terrified of dying—Boswell may exaggerate this a little, but there is evidence enough from other sources, including Johnson's own prayers and meditations. After all, a due circumspection was called for on the simplest and most rational grounds: 'You know (says he), I never thought confidence with respect to futurity any part of the character of a brave, a wise or a good man. Bravery has no place where it can avail nothing' (B 4. 395). So as we read of his hard-won acceptance of his approaching dissolution, sustained by his 'late conversion', we are more impressed than we should be if he had possessed the insouciance of a Hume. His refusal to take any opiates is symbolic of his entire moral being: anything was preferable in his eyes to an unexamined life or an inability to face reality.

It is doubly apt that Thomas Carlyle should have consecrated Johnson in the role of hero as man of letters. First, because the works from Johnson's pen testify to an indomitable spirit and provide models of clear and cogent writing. Secondly, because his literary career shows us how a hand-to-mouth professional existence can be ennobled into a high vocation. J. S. Cunningham has said of *Rasselas* that 'the book is telling us, without any false assurances, to *live* ... It will not be, in any event, absolute felicity; but knowing that to be so is not an occasion for despair.' That formulation might serve as a motto to much of Johnson's work. The books he wrote and the life he led can still endow us with the courage to *be*.

Further reading

There is a vast library surrounding Johnson. The selective list which follows is limited to standard editions and major studies, including some of the most influential monographs on particular topics (place of publication is London, unless otherwise shown).

Works

The standard edition in progress is *The Yale Edition of the Works of Samuel Johnson* (New Haven, Conn., 1958–   ). So far thirteen volumes have appeared, including those devoted to the poems, the periodical essays, the edition of Shakespeare, the *Journey to the Western Islands*, the political writings, and *Rasselas*. A widely used earlier edition is that of the *Works*, ed. Arthur Murphy, 12 vols. (1792, often reprinted).

There are good editions of individual works, including *The Lives of the Poets*, ed. G. B. Hill, 3 vols. (Oxford, 1905; repr. Hildesheim, 1968), and *The Life of Savage*, ed. C. Tracy (Oxford, 1971). The *Prefaces and Dedications* have been edited by A. T. Hazen (New Haven, Conn., 1937). The best edition of the *Journey to the Western Islands* is that of J. D. Fleeman (Oxford, 1985); the same scholar has produced a useful text of *The Complete English Poems* (Harmondsworth, 1971). For a handy selection, see *Johnson on Shakespeare*, ed. H. R. Woudhuysen (Harmondsworth, 1989).

Among many useful anthologies, the most accessible is a volume on Johnson for the Oxford Authors, ed. D. Greene (Oxford, 1984). For personal items, see *Johnson on Johnson*, ed. J. Wain (1976).

The Standard edition of the *Letters* is by R. W. Chapman, 3 vols. (Oxford, 1952). B. Redford is preparing a new edition: vols. 1–3, covering the years to 1781, appeared in 1992.

Biography

Boswell's *Life of Johnson* exists in numerous forms: the standard edition is by G. B. Hill and L. F. Powell, 6 vols. (Oxford, 1934–64); this also contains Boswell's *Tour of the Hebrides*. There is a one-volume World's Classics edition of the complete *Life*, ed. R. W. Chapman and J. D. Fleeman (Oxford, 1980).

Other classic accounts are those of Hester Thrale, whose *Anecdotes* of Johnson have been edited by A. Sherbo (1974); and John Hawkins, whose *Life* has been abridged and edited by B. H. Davis (1962). A great amount of material is also to be found in *Johnsonian Miscellanies*, ed. G. B. Hill, 2 vols. (Oxford, 1897), and *Thraliana*, ed. K. C. Balderston, 2 vols. (Oxford, 2nd edn. 1951). The minor early biographies have been collectively edited by R. E. Kelley and O M Brack (Iowa City, Ia., 1974).

Among modern biographies, the most important are: J. L. Clifford, *Young Samuel Johnson* (1955) and *Dictionary Johnson* (1980), carrying the story as far as 1763; J. Wain, *Samuel Johnson* (1974); and W. J. Bate, *Samuel Johnson* (1978). See also T. Kaminski, *The Early Career of Samuel Johnson* (New York, NY, 1987). N. Page, *A Johnson Chronology* (1990) is a useful, though far from complete, record of day-to-day activities.

Bibliography

The standard work of reference is W. P. Courtney and D. Nichol Smith, *A Bibliography of Samuel Johnson* (Oxford, 1915; repr. 1968). This should be supplemented by J. L. Clifford and D. J. Greene, *Samuel Johnson: A Survey and Bibliography of Critical Studies* (Minneapolis, Minn., 1970). A more recent update is D. J. Greene and J. A. Vance, *A Bibliography of Johnsonian Studies 1970–85* (Victoria, BC, 1987).

J. D. Fleeman has produced editions of Johnson's manuscripts and books associated with him, as well as the sale catalogue of his books; D. J. Greene has written an annotated guide to his library.

Critical studies

There are several good general guides to Johnson's career and thought; the most perceptive remains W. J. Bate, *The Achievement of Samuel Johnson* (New York, NY, 1955); the most dependable recent treatment is J. P. Hardy, *Samuel Johnson: A Critical Study* (1979), along with the provocative and vigorous book by Donald Greene, *Samuel Johnson* (New York, NY, rev. edn. 1989).

Almost every corner of Johnson's thought has been given specialized attention, but some individual monographs of marked importance are these: C. F. Chapin, *The Religious Thought of Samuel Johnson* (Ann Arbor, Mich., 1968); T. M. Curley, *Samuel Johnson and the Age of Travel* (Athens, Ga., 1975); R. Folkenflik, *Samuel Johnson Biographer* (Ithaca, NY, 1978); D. J. Greene, *The Politics of Samuel Johnson* (New Haven, Conn., 1960; rev. edn., Athens, Ga., 1990); J. Wiltshire, *Samuel Johnson in the Medical World* (Cambridge, 1991); J. H. Hagstrum, *Samuel Johnson's Literary Criticism* (Minneapolis, Minn., 1952; rev. edn., Chicago, Ill., 1967); C. McIntosh, *The Choice of Life: Samuel Johnson and the World of Fiction* (New Haven, Conn., 1973); M. J. Quinlan, *Samuel Johnson: A Layman's Religion* (Madison, Wis., 1964); J. A. Vance, *Samuel Johnson and the Sense of History* (Athens, Ga., 1984); and two books by W. K. Wimsatt: *The Prose Style of Samuel Johnson* (New Haven, Conn., 1941) and *Philosophic Words* (New Haven, Conn., 1948). Wider matters are discussed in A. Kernan, *Printing Technology, Letters and Samuel Johnson* (Princeton, NJ, 1987). A controversial, and to some unsuccessful, attempt to show that Johnson possessed greater taste in the arts, other than literature, than he has usually been granted is that of M. Brownell, *Samuel Johnson's Attitude to the Arts* (Oxford, 1989). A good picture of Johnson's intellectual and theological context is provided by N. Hudson, *Samuel Johnson and Eighteenth-Century Thought* (Oxford, 1988).

The best study to date of the Shakespearian criticism is G. F. Parker, *Johnson's Shakespeare* (Oxford, 1989). On the *Dictionary*, see R. DeMaria, Jr., *Johnson's Dictionary and the Language of Learning* (Oxford, 1986); A. Reddick, *The Making of Johnson's Dictionary 1746–1773* (Cambridge, 1990); and J. H. Sledd and G. J. Kolb, *Dr Johnson's Dictionary: Essays in the Biography of a Book* (Chicago, Ill., 1955). For the sermons, see J. Gray, *Johnson's Sermons: A Study* (Oxford, 1972). R. B. Schwartz, *Samuel Johnson and the New Science* (Madison, Wis., 1971), is an effective treatment of Johnson's scientific interests.

The most successful attempt to place Johnson's thought in the wider context of developments in taste is still that of W. J. Bate, *From Classic to Romantic* (Cambridge, Mass., 1946). The fullest survey of the milieu in which Johnson operated, even though it is now a little dated, remains *Johnson's England*, ed. A. S. Turberville, 2 vols. (Oxford, 1933).

Index

115